Group Spirituality

Group Spirituality is an increasingly popular area of focus, and working in groups raises some very different and valuable consequences which wouldn't necessarily arise in a one-to-one encounter. In *Group Spirituality*, Roger Grainger, an author already established as an authority on Dramatherapy, provides a practical guide to group spirituality and workshops.

Derived from the author's experiences of working with groups of people interested in exploring their own and other people's spirituality, *Group Spirituality* turns an abstract idea into a practical and recognizable experience. The nature of group work, the embodiment of ideas and feelings, and circumstances aiding personal encounter are discussed. Workshop examples aimed at establishing group identity and the introduction of the idea of the 'safe place' are explained. The symbolism of spiritual awareness is approached, and a firm distinction between spirituality and religion is made.

Group Spirituality's approach to spirituality from a workshop focus, successfully attempts to embody spirituality and provide a framework for consciously examining and integrating spirituality within the rest of our lives.

Roger Grainger is a chartered counselling psychologist and parish minister, who formerly worked as chaplain of Stanley Royd Psychiatric Hospital in Wakefield. He combines professional theatre work with writing and teaching, and is the author of several books about worship and therapy.

Group Spirituality

A Workshop Approach

Roger Grainger

Brunner-Routledge
Taylor & Francis Group

HOVE AND NEW YORK

First published 2003
by Brunner-Routledge
27 Church Road, Hove, East Sussex BN3 2FA

Simultaneously published in the USA and Canada
by Brunner-Routledge
29 West 35th Street, New York NY 10001

Brunner-Routledge is an imprint of the Taylor & Francis Group

© 2003 Roger Grainger

Typeset in Times by Keystroke, Jacaranda Lodge, Wolverhampton
Printed and bound in Great Britain by MPG Books Ltd, Bodmin, Cornwall
Paperback cover design by Richard Massing

British Library Cataloguing in Publication Data
A catalogue record for this book is available from the British Library

Library of Congress Cataloging in Publication Data
Grainger, Roger.
  Group spirituality: a workshop approach / Roger Grainger.
     p. cm.
  ISBN 1-58391-917-1 (pbk. : alk. paper) – ISBN 1-58391-916-3 (hbk :
alk. paper)
     1. Small groups–Religious aspects. 2. Spiritual life. I. Title.
BL628.4.G73 2003
291.4′46–dc21
                                     2002155881

ISBN 1–58391–916–3 (hbk)
ISBN 1–58391–917–1 (pbk)

for Zoya Zuvcenko

Contents

Figures

Acknowledgement

I would like to thank Stanley and Elizabeth Baxter and the community of Holy Rood House for all they have done to make the writing of this book possible.

Preface

It may seem a little strange for an actor to be writing a preface for a book about spirituality. When you think about it, however, it really isn't strange at all. After all, drama is about being human; about the ways in which we share thoughts, feelings and experiences which concern us all. Some of these may be light hearted, certainly. Others go deeper, some to the very roots of our humanness.

Roger Grainger's book looks at ways in which groups of people can use drama and the dramatic imagination to create scenarios in which people may explore the things which concern us all very deeply, by giving themselves permission to make real use of their 'as if' abilities and benefit from the result.

You don't have to be able to act in order to enjoy these workshops, although you may find you're more of an actor than you thought you were. They are what they say they are – workshops, not performances. They come from Roger Grainger's experience over many years, working as a dramatherapist with groups of people of all kinds, some of whom were completely new to 'this sort of thing', and not a little scared by the prospect of being involved in it. They were surprised by the way it helped them to get things into perspective with regard to what being human actually meant to them in their life among other people, sharing and growing in their company.

Which is what 'spirituality' means here.

Richard Briers

Prologue

I asked the group what spirituality was. This is what they said.

- Something beyond.
- A source of wholeness.
- Something to hope for.
- Trusting it's all worthwhile.
- Having faith when you can't really prove things.
- Going deeper.
- Going home.
- Going there.

Tell me more, I said, go further, and they did.

- It's belonging.
- Accepting.
- Blessing.
- Goodness.
- Being really fair.
- Trusting people.
- Something behind all this, able to make sense of it.
- Things adding up.
- The real meaning.
- Hope.
- Peace.
- Inner comfort.
- Innerness itself.
- Depth and height.

What does it feel like, then?

- Being involved in something that's good in a way I can't express.
- A sense of crossing a threshold.
- It's a quality of height, breadth and depth which both contains and liberates. It holds me safe and sets me free.
- What you don't expect.

Can you feel it here? Is it the sort of thing that can happen in a group? Like this one?

- Oh yes, they said.

Introduction

This book arose from my experience of working with groups who were interested in exploring their own and other people's spirituality, either because they sensed that it would be relevant to their work as nurses, teachers, social workers, leaders of church congregations, etc., or because they felt personally inspired to do so. It aims to show how members of a particular kind of group, the Spirituality workshop, may work together. I begin by considering insights arising from the nature of the group work itself, particularly the holistic experience of a shared identity among group members. This part of the book (Chapter 1) introduces some ideas and topics which will be expanded later (e.g. embodiment of ideas and feelings, use of personal stories, need for and use of structure) and ends with examples of workshops aimed at establishing group identity. The following chapter (Chapter 2) probes more deeply into the circumstances which permit personal encounter, and introduces the idea of a 'safe place' for exploring the ways in which we interact with one another. The structure of the group allows us to rediscover our ability to play together: important things about being human – spiritual values – are approached and shared in ways experienced as secure and unthreatening. The chapter ends as before, with examples of workshops designed to explore this kind of 'distancing' effect.

Chapter 3 is concerned with the symbolism of spiritual awareness, and moves into areas associated with experience that is avowedly spiritual (i.e. defined as such). A distinction is made between spirituality and religion, while preserving the understanding that both concern a quality of experience that is self-validating and transpersonal – a shared journey, in fact – and this is the form taken by the workshops at the end of the chapter.

The next chapter (Chapter 4) brings us back to the everyday experience of otherness which we encounter in dreams. The workshops here are designed to make an essentially individual and 'private' experience available for sharing, concentrating on the frightening aspects of encounter with the unknown, and the group's ability to 'take trauma into itself' and contribute to the healing of emotionally wounded people. The book ends with a return to the beginning – Chapter 5 concentrates upon creation myths. Its workshops aim at restoring to us a sense of the primal reality of being, thus bringing the wheel full circle.

Spirituality is often regarded as if it were exclusively individual, if not actually a private concern, and a great deal has been written about it from this point of view. Experience with groups shows that this is not necessarily the case (cf Durkheim!). There is consequently a need to make the connection between the transpersonal awareness of group experience, as this is understood by social psychologists, psychotherapists and other specialists in group work, and the overtly spiritual approach of religious people. This book approaches the idea of spirituality from two directions – the spirituality of personal encounter and group sharing, and the spirituality of inspired imagination. It is therefore particularly relevant for professionals who have, up to now, been disposed by inclination or training to discount spirituality, regarding it as irrelevant to their way of working, but are now increasingly drawn to take account of its significance as a vital part of the status quo with regard to almost every kind of human context. Like it or not, spirituality is a fact of life.

I have to say at the very beginning, however, that this book is not about spirituality as such. It doesn't attempt to explain what spirituality is, for instance. Spirituality is something experienced rather than described. That is why the kind of group discussed here is more like a workshop than an ordinary learning group. Nor is it a book about groups as such. The group exercises described here attempt to provide a structure for personal encounter in which those taking part are encouraged to relax their hold upon the urge to take up a defensive position with regard to themselves and other people, and use their imagination to explore alternative ways of relating to one another within a specially contrived environment which is both psychologically safe and spiritually challenging. The way they do this is much more like art than science; and the kind of art is an improvised drama.

Each of the groups described here is different from the others. Each emerged from a different set of circumstances. There is no set of rules with regard to the number and duration of sessions, number or selection of members, choice of subject matter, or style of leadership, although enthusiasm for what is going on in the workshop is *sine qua non* for all of them. There is no scientifically acceptable way of telling whether or not they have 'worked', or indeed what 'working' means under these circumstances. Perhaps the best way of doing this would be to measure them against one or other of the statements included in the Prologue to this book as attempts at defining spirituality.

The structural elements involved in this kind of workshop will, of course, be described later. They are in fact very simple, so much so that workshops of this kind can easily be put together and certainly require no special training. This is, in fact, why the book was written – to demonstrate the simplicity and availability of this kind of workshop approach, so that others might develop it in their own way, to fit their own requirements. Once the reader has got the hang of this approach, I recommend her or him to try it out. First of all, however, they would need to understand the underlying principles of what is being done here. The idea of exploring spirituality within a group setting suggests people turned outwards from themselves towards one another. The idea of exploring spirituality in this way suggests the experience of those engaged in searching for an answer to the question 'What does it mean to be human?' These are not 'just' workshops, any more than the groups involved are just groups. There is a key element involved here, lying in the way that these workshops are put together – the way they are *structured*.

The kind of structure used here is artistic rather than instrumental. That is, the workshops do not consist of people doing and saying things connected with a particular agenda which they have agreed together and know how to achieve. They will not teach anyone here to 'be spiritual', or even, in precise terms, what spirituality actually is. Instead, they move obliquely towards the meanings they express. Those involved, including the leader, do not know what will emerge in the way of feelings or ideas. In a sense they do not want to know this, being content to set out in the direction of an answer to a question that has not yet been asked, or not asked directly. As in drama (which sometimes comes into play here), the real question emerges during the course of the action. Because it is a fundamental question, one about what life and death really mean, it cannot be asked in any other way without reducing its significance. Those taking part in the workshop collude in order to 'tell the story slant', agreeing to use their imagination and construct a shared world, one they have made up for themselves, which could indeed be theirs but isn't – or not in a way they will usually acknowledge.

In the spirituality workshop, however, this dangerous story becomes our own. The structure of the workshop makes it safe for us to inhabit it, bringing to it our own personal reality, the things we would ordinarily keep hidden, or at least shelve for the time being. I will suggest that it is the relationship between structure and freedom that makes this kind of experience liberating, in the same way that drama is liberating. The world we invent together, using our imagination to do so, is safe enough for us to take some chances in. Because what we have put together is 'only imagination', and not reality at all, we can bring our own reality into it.

These workshops are usually constructed like stories or plays, with a beginning, a middle and an end. The first part aims at establishing a sense of security. It tells us the kind of thing we are in for while at the same time assuring us of our safety, that it is not in fact a story specially made up about *us* however much we may think it is; so that by the middle we have allowed ourselves to become really involved and are caught up in its world, having to be brought back in the final part into the world of our own everyday concerns. This use of shared imagination makes it safe for us to get involved with the implications of being human in a way we often avoid, consequently expanding our own humanness.

The workshops aim to do three things

1 to establish a feeling of safety, making it possible for those taking part
2 to move into the 'as if' mode in order to explore areas of experience which would cause us to feel anxiety about ourselves and then
3 to bring us back home again by reflecting upon the significance of the world we have been imagining with regard to our own every day lives.

'Safe' – 'As if' – 'Reflection'. This experience of balanced danger and safety is, of course, by no means confined to spirituality workshops. Its connection with Aristotle's theory of catharsis is obvious (Scheff 1979) and it is familiar to students of group process. Oatley, for instance, reminds us that 'One structure which groups and individual therapy seeks to provide is a structure of simultaneous support and challenge.' This, he tells us, is essential for 'experiential therapeutic learning' (1984: 127). This experience of safety-in-danger defies attempts at quantification. It is also extremely difficult (if not impossible) to reproduce, except perhaps artistically – and art is well known for its ability to speak to different people in different ways. If spirituality is characterised by its elusiveness, both as concept and experience, then cathartic freedom to engage, in the way revealed by these workshops, is genuinely spiritual.

The workshops themselves are definite enough, however. From one point of view they are the most important part of the book, the rest of it providing background material in the form of supportive theories which throw light on their action. The first part of each chapter attempts to put the reader in touch with some of the thinking that went into their design, or may, in some cases, have emerged from it. These parts of the book tend, perhaps, to be a little abstract. If they do, then by all means turn first to the workshops themselves, the records of actual events, because it is the practicality of this approach that matters. Spirituality is an experience, not a theoretical construct; sometimes psychological theories and aesthetic doctrine are a not very convincing attempt to explain the inexplicable.

A word of explanation may be called for about the connection between spirituality itself, whatever that self may be, and the 'existential therapeutic learning' associated with this kind of workshop approach. For the purpose of these workshops, spirituality may be defined as the awareness of an existential movement 'between' and 'beyond' which is experienced as self-transcendence, the crossing of existential boundaries. These workshops represent a particular way in which people become aware of this kind of experience. Obviously there are other ways too, some of them involving the use of therapeutic groups. Although this is not a book about spirituality as such, it may perhaps be seen as providing evidence for one way of defining the spiritual. This is the 'transpersonal' approach which originated in the thought of C.G. Jung and was developed by writers such as John Washburn (1995) and Stanislav Grof (1979). According to transpersonal psychology, although human beings have this kind of separate existence and can to some extent be studied as individuals, their spiritual reality includes any form of separateness. 'There is' says Wilber, 'but one self, taking on these different outward forms, for every person has the identical intuition of the same inner I-ness transcending the body' (1985; 134). This 'intuition of the single Self' is what we recognise as spirituality; in other words a transcendental reality uniting all human beings and our yearning for the spiritual. It is contacted via the imagination and expressed in the form of works of art. Mythological thinking, which uses images and narratives rather than logical argument, far from being 'primitive' and 'anti-scientific', is the most convincing evidence about the human psyche's growth towards a creative synthesis.

All this, of course, is highly synthetic. The significance of trans-personal psychology for this book lies in the fact that it provides an explanation, in terms of a recognizable tradition of psychological enquiry, of our awareness of truths which lie beyond our intellectual grasp. From the point of view of spiritual experience itself, however, it remains an attempt to explain the inexplicable. Theory has certainly been extended but experience has not, and the more inclusive the theoretical explanation of spiritual experience, the greater the gap between the experience itself and our success in explaining it away. In group situations such as those described here, those involved were engaged in the attempt to explore ideas and feelings associated with our private strivings for answers to questions that go on defying precise formulation, which have now become identifiable moments within the histories of particular groups of people – moments which, for those involved, possessed spiritual resonance.

The spirituality of workshops is implicit within their action. It is quite definite, though, in the sense that the workshops are focused on particular ideas or themes used as opportunities for spiritual experience. The workshops came first; the chapter titles refer in the first place to them, and only secondarily to other things mentioned within the chapters, which sometimes touch upon areas not obviously connected with spirituality, but which are always enriched by being drawn into its orbit.

This is not intended to be a systematic treatment of spirituality, which is always to some extent a contradiction in terms. Nor is it intended to suggest that the only way to approach the subject is via this kind of workshop. My intention throughout has been to share some of the excitement I personally find in working in this way. Wherever the subject matter is difficult, whenever it is painful or elusive, whenever it concerns the inner life of individuals or groups, wherever it is perceived as fundamentally important and demands special attention – to work within this format is frequently to be both illuminated and spiritually enriched. Nowadays there is a growing number of people who are searching for ways in which to achieve genuine contact with their own and other people's ideas and feelings. Many well-established professions which are rooted in, and consequently confined by, direct approaches to teaching and learning, and are skilled in techniques of 'dealing with' situations involving people, are searching for ways to bring life into old, dry bones by growth in spiritual awareness. They are beginning to feel that the ways they go about explaining life may actually be out of touch with the way people really think about its meaning and significance. For generations, even centuries, they have left such things to others, content to stick to their own last, and practise their own well-tried expertise. Now, however, they are not so sure.

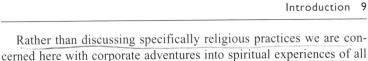

Rather than discussing specifically religious practices we are concerned here with corporate adventures into spiritual experiences of all kinds. It certainly speaks to religious people, both individuals and congregations, but not exclusively to them. All who believe there to be a spiritual dimension to life, and want to explore their perceptions with others, will find encouragement here. It is not a textbook either, but rather a record of spiritual moments – a book of inspirations in fact. The main contribution it sets out to make to the literature about spirituality lies in the fact that the inspiration is structured within the context of specific events with the life experiences of those taking part.

Thus the book is addressed to a range of people – doctors, teachers, social workers, psychologists and psychotherapists, both students and practitioners; people involved in business and administration; group workers of every kind. Its obvious appeal is to leaders of church congregations; but it is open to other professions too. Nurses in particular are becoming increasingly concerned about the spiritual dimension of their work, as shown by the growing number of books and articles on the subject which have been appearing over the last few years. The aim of the workshop approach is to make exploration into spirituality available to all, not simply to specialists in group work.

This, I think, is the thing about this book which distinguishes it from other treatments of the subject. There are certainly books about spirituality, and there may be some about the spirituality of groups (although I am not aware of them); but I am reasonably sure that none of these is based on a workshop approach, and certainly not one of the tried and tested kind presented here. In many trials taking place over the years I have found the workshop approach to be flexible and inclusive. It is specifically designed to promote spontaneity and to avoid imposing any one point of view – even the leader's!

Chapter 1

The spirituality of groups

1   Sit or stand somewhere in the room. (Talk if you want!) When the leader calls you, come and stand in a circle with the others.

2   Say who you are to the person on each side of you. Now say why you have come to the workshop (just one of the reasons, please).

3   Listen to the leader as she/he reads Mary Coleridge's poem *Soul-Gibberish* (1908).

> Many a flower have I seen blossom,
>   Many a bird for me will sing.
> Never heard I so sweet a singer,
>   Never saw I so fair a thing.
>
> She is a bird, a bird that blossoms,
>   She is a flower, a flower that sings;
> And I a flower when I behold her,
>   And when I hear her, I have wings.

4   Explore the room by yourself. See what you can find that takes your eye. As you go, try to remember the poem. What do you think it means? Does it mean anything to you?

5   Come back to the circle again. Now follow the leader's instructions. They will start some simple group exercises to help you relax and 'settle in' to the workshop.

Leader   First of all, let's stand (or sit) in as relaxed a way as we can. Now imagine that it's a lovely warm day. The sun is shining, and there's just a faint breath of a breeze, so relax as much as you can and enjoy it. Drink the air, drink it in as deep as you can. . . . Begin to feel the first drops of rain – warm rain falling gently on your forehead. Lift your face to meet it. As it gets heavier, open yourself out to it.

... Now you are drenched, soaked to the skin. Take
an imaginary towel and dry somebody with it. Rub them
down. Now let them do the same to you.

6   When you feel warm and dry, sit in the circle and listen to the music.
Someone reads whilst you are listening

I am not a mechanism, an assembly of various sections
And it is not because the mechanism is working wrongly that I
    am ill.
I am ill because of wounds to the soul, to the deep emotional
    self –
and the wounds to the soul take a long time,
only time can help, and patience
and a certain difficult repentance, a long difficult repentance,
realisation of life's mistakes, and the freeing oneself
from the endless repetition of the mistake
which mankind at large has chosen to sanctify.
                        'Healing', D.H. Lawrence by permission

7   Find yourself a partner; explore with them to discover a space where
you can sit or stand so you are facing each other. Make yourselves
comfortable in the space you have found. If you like you can sit on
cushions. Spend some time listening to the music. When you are
ready

a   say what it is like to be here, now go a bit deeper
b   say what it is like to be a woman or a man (whichever you are)
c   now say what it is like to be a person.

8   Light one of the small candles and place it on the floor between you.
9   Hold hands round your candle.
10 Rejoin the main group in a circle and hold hands. Gently squeeze the
hand of the person on your right. Do this in turn, so that the squeeze
is passed round the circle until it comes back to you.
11 Divide into two groups. If somebody asked you what 'spirituality'
was, how would you answer? Make a living picture of what
'spirituality' might be, using everybody in your group. This can
involve movement if you wish, or it can be a kind of stillness – or it
can be both. Here are some examples

a   a rose (or another kind of flower)
b   a river

c a pathway
d a mountain
e a forest, etc.

12 Show what you have made to the other group.
13 Sit in the circle again. After being quiet for a few moments, share some of your thoughts with the group.
14 Say goodbye to everybody, spending a little time with your partner. Who's going to take the candle? (Who's going to give it?)

The above was a workshop that took place at the AGM Conference of the British Association for Dramatherapists, York University, 1993. Participants were drama and arts therapists from several parts of the world.

I, thou, we

Reflexivity and inter-relatedness as fundamental human experience.

Who am I? Who do *you* think I am?
As human beings we are characteristically unable to contemplate ourselves without taking some account of other people – either their presence or absence. At a basic level, to be human is to be in some way *related*. Human relationship involves three dimensions of awareness

- I and my experience of everything (including myself)
- you and your experience of everything (including yourself)
- a dimension involving me-as-you (when I put myself in your shoes, as it were) and you-as-me (when you do the same with regard to me), the two processes being alternative aspects of the same shared experience of personhood.

This latter dimension has been described in several ways, as 'inter-subjective reflexivity', empathy, 'shared imagination' and 'projective identification', each of which is a way of describing the experience of psychological sharing of personhood. There are thus three complementary realms – mine, yours, ours – in which the third aspect of humanness can be seen as binding the other two together, while at the same time liberating them from captivity to themselves and turning them outward towards otherness and one another.

Working in groups serves as a powerful reminder both of our corporality – the things we share, both as bodies and as *a* body – and also our individuality, or what we think of as being unique to ourselves. Logically speaking, of course, this is a paradox, because we usually think of these things as opposites. In practice, however, it turns out to be quite straightforward: when we are aware of the presence of others we are also most conscious of ourselves as distinct from the rest. Crowds tend to prevent people from speaking up for themselves. Groups, on the other hand, encourage them to do so.

At a higher level of abstraction, groups can be seen as structures for extending the kind of sharing which constitutes the primary condition of personal relationship, so that its nature and effects can be explored and enjoyed by the people taking part. To put this another way, the threefold experience of sharing – mine, yours, ours – is the primary human group. This notion that fundamental personal reality is threefold, and that in personal terms threeness is an ultimate category of being, is established within the doctrinal structure of important world religions, notably Christianity and Hinduism (Pannikar 1973), a fact which has important implications with regard to the spiritual nature of group experience.

The fact that, by definition, groups contain more than two people does not necessarily make them less personal. The group is essentially a context for sharing a structure for relationship. Just as actors require an audience of other persons (and will actually imagine they have one if necessary) so human persons of all kinds require the presence of others – or at least of an other – to reflect their reality and give depth to their experience of themselves and each other. Relationship and reflexivity go together; personal reality cannot exist out of context.

The spirituality of a group can best be described as what it is that makes a group able to communicate with itself in ways that defy analysis. Group spirituality is the unseen presence within the group that makes it into a healing context for relationship.

2 + 2 = ?

Group holisms.

Trust the group process, let it go on . . . in the group we're wiser than we know.

(Carl Rogers, video training seminar with counsellors, Illinois University, 1973)

There's something that rises up in me, and I've learned to trust it; my behaviour is quite different when I'm in a group from the way it is in individual therapy, and this is because of what I've learned on groups.

(ibid.)

We are wiser than we know. Talking spontaneously on a training video, Carl Rogers reveals what is perhaps a basic truth about the experience of human groups. It is part of his understanding of what he describes as 'group process'. In some way or other, the group is able to know things *as a group*. This group wisdom is distinct from that of any single member. In fact, as Rogers implies, it is a different kind of knowing. When we are in a group we both feel and act differently from the way we do on other occasions and in other places. At least, this is how it seems to us. Our experience of ourselves and of other people is different within the group. It is not merely some kind of subtle difference, a slight variation in atmosphere, calling for the simple adjustment of one's state of mind. Or at least, it may have subtle reasons, but its effects are certainly quite definite, or even powerfully distinct.

Sometimes they are uncomfortably powerful, so that one's psychological repose is violently shattered, and with it one's view of oneself as an experienced person, well trained to deal with interpersonal events, even unexpected ones. Nothing very much seems to have happened to interfere with the normal course of events in the exterior world – you are accustomed to sitting in an ordinary room, with a group of people you've already met, some of whom you may actually know quite well; indeed, the circumstances have a familiar air about them, carrying vague memories of various kinds of social groups, relaxed occasions when you have exchanged stories and swapped reminiscences. You know this is going to be different, of course. What you don't know is *how* different.

The following are extracts from a journal kept by a male member of a group set up to explore its own members' experience. A psychologist – the Process Observer – was also present.

Week I Why isn't anyone saying anything? Is this woman (i.e. the Process Observer) a group member or not? . . . There's a feeling of all being in the same boat, of having similar feelings. It seems to be an 'us-against-her' feeling (referring to the PO). Being on the defensive seems to stop people saying anything. She has drawn us together, I think. But I must do something to contribute more.

Week II I began to enjoy the feeling of sharing the group's discomfort.

Week IV During this session I was reminded of the very painful experience I had had in a training group a year previously. Like the present group, that one had also consisted entirely of women. This fact suddenly came to me with great force – and I found myself telling the group about it. No-one seemed to object. If somebody admits to being upset, the others will be supportive.

Week V I was conscious of an anger I shared with the group. Nobody seemed able to say anything. How much longer is this going on?

Week VI A group member said she felt we were all tied up in a game we didn't know the rules for. There was a lot of agreement, mainly unspoken. The Process Observer said we were behaving like adolescents – immediate outbursts of silent anger in the group. Suddenly it felt much easier to talk. Even the Process Observer seemed more human.

Week VII I felt the group helped me face some things about the way I relate to others. The group felt more fragmented this week.

Week IX A feeling of security, all in it together. PO drew attention to dialogue between X (another group member) and me; perhaps the others had felt left out? They said they hadn't felt this. A member said she felt 'maternal' towards the group, and the Process Observer commented that she thought the group was 'inclusive, perhaps'.

Week X Self-pity, anger, frustration. I fell asleep halfway through – an event later described by PO as expressing 'a feeling of weariness in the group', of being 'drained of energy'. She said I was acting this out on behalf of everyone else. When I wakened up I felt something which I experienced as portraying the feelings of the entire group against myself. This brought with it a powerful memory of the incident referred to in Week IV. I felt rejected and hopeless.

The purpose of including this material is to draw attention to the relationship between the feelings of an individual member of the group and the sense he had of a shared 'group feeling'. Most of the time he was involved in this shared experience; sometimes, however, he was extremely conscious of being subjected to it in the role of an outsider, almost a victim. There was a degree of objective, circumstantial, justification for feeling this, of course, because of the actual constitution of the group in which he was bound to be the 'odd man out'; and at this junction of his personal life he felt he had reasons for being wary of groups consisting entirely of women. The victimisation he felt was the mirror image of the acceptance he enjoyed earlier, however. In fact, the most outstanding feature of this group was the extent to which feelings were shared.

The group took place during the first ten weeks of what was, to most of the people taking part, a new course. Certainly, these six people had never worked together before. It was customary for them to spend the first part of the afternoon struggling with material that was difficult for them to understand, and certainly made some, perhaps all, of them feel confused, and consequently inadequate. The effect of this, I think, can be seen in a note jotted down by this particular member:

> We have a way of being together – close, sensing one another's defensiveness, hiding behind our anonymity as group members, glad when one of us admits to being at a loss, and *letting them speak for the group*. In this way individual competence need not be examined and our own weakness exposed. (my italics)

What showed itself in the group was, at its worst, defensiveness and mutual protection; at its best, what Tillich calls 'the courage to be *as a part*' (1962a, my italics).

In his work on the group process, Carl Rogers expresses his faith in the capacity of a group to move on its own initiative. The group process moves towards a positive, therapeutic, outcome because human beings *themselves* 'move towards wholeness and self-actualisation' (Corey 2000). In other words, therapeutic groups express and embody the underlying tendency towards psychological wholeness present in each of the individuals that comprise them. The movement is from non-being to being, from meaninglessness to meaning. The experience of group membership helps us to question values we never doubted before and to discover new aspects of ourselves, thus reconciling conflicting elements in our understanding of life, so that we feel ourselves engaged in a personal universe to which we contribute and by which we are validated (cf. Corey 2000). The idea of a creative group process goes back to the beginning of the study of group psychology. It has always been recognised that there is 'a formative tendency' in the process itself (Yalom *et al.* 1973).

For example, Tuckman describes stages ('forming', 'storming', 'norming' and 'performing')[1] through which groups must pass on the way to working together effectively and producing real changes within a shared environment (1965). At each of these stages the group is affected in four areas: structure, task process, leadership and interpersonal process. All develop in different ways as the group itself gradually changes its overall identity. In this way a group moves from being an ad hoc collection of individuals to 'an entity capable of diagnosing and solving problems and making decisions' (Fay and Doyle 1982). In this condition of interdependence and mutual support, the members use the sense of achievement at having made the group 'work' to give themselves the courage required finally to close it down.

The idea that therapeutic groups have a developing life of their own was explored in depth by writers of the psychodynamic school of group therapy. Freud himself had maintained that the psychology of individuals was a function of the relationship between one person and another (1930). Foulkes, writing more than thirty years later, saw group processes as 'primary elements' within the experience of the group which could not be explained solely in terms of the interaction taking place among individuals (1965). In this he differed from Bion, who was not willing to go so far towards any suggestion that the whole was 'greater than the sum of its parts', and spoke instead of

> valency – a spontaneous, unconscious function of the gregarious quality in the personality of man. The apparent difference between group psychology and individual psychology is an illusion produced by the fact that the group brings into prominence phenomena that appear alien to an observer unaccustomed to using the group.
>
> (1961: 169–170)

All the same, ideas of group holism, of an experience 'greater than the sum of its parts' flourished in other branches of psychotherapy. I myself have been conscious during experiential group sessions of a quality of an awareness which was somehow brought about by belonging to the group, and yet was subtly different from ideas and feelings I had *about* the group, even ones I had about being a member of it myself. The best way I can describe this is as a sensation of being in touch with a source of understanding of a kind that is experienced without being actually understood. This acted as a kind of prompting presence, a voice

---

1 The model was later extended to take in a final stage, that of 'adjourning'.

behind people's voices, something which individuals spoke *on behalf of* with a confidence beyond the scope of ordinary empathy. Being in a group increases our awareness of shared ideas and feelings at the level described by Bion as 'basic assumptions'. These are primitive techniques of self-preservation working to simplify and exaggerate feelings in a way and to a degree unlikely to be found in other kinds of social setting. Nevertheless, there is something else too, something more generous, less driven than this. The group expands people's awareness, as well as exaggerating their basic needs for safety and libidinal satisfaction.

This seems to me to be what Rogers means when he says that in the group 'we're wiser than we know' (1970). It is not always a comfortable kind of knowledge; it doesn't add up to the sort of thing you can easily describe either to your self or anyone else. On the level of people's ordinary ways of making sense of things, there may seem to be a frustrating absence of progress. On another level, however, something quite different is happening; the intensified awareness of one another's feelings gives a weird sense of movement taking place within the group – a kind of corporate progress, not willed but certainly experienced. Another member of the group already mentioned put it like this 'It's as if we're all on a journey together, but I don't know where to'. Certainly it may never become more explicit than this. All the same it is exploratory rather than simply defensive; a journey *towards*. This kind of knowledge is learned through, and transmitted by, the group. It is characterised by individual understanding which is only available through group experience.

The development of psychodynamic theory, which has the most to contribute so far as a theoretical understanding of this kind of group wisdom is concerned, seems to have been not group analysis but psychodrama. Describing his work with groups of patients, Moreno tells how he

> began to emphasise the moment, the dynamics of the moment, the warming up to the moment . . . not only from the point of view of philosophy and phenomenology, but from the point of view of the therapeutic process as it takes place in connection with patients and within patient groups.
>
> (Moreno 1969, cited in Fox 1987: 4)

Moreno calls the process of communication 'tele', 'The fundamental process of *tele* is reciprocity – reciprocity of action, reciprocity of rejection, reciprocity of excitation, reciprocity of inhibition, reciprocity of indifference, reciprocity of distortion.' (ibid.) It is precisely because we find ourselves in the same close psychodynamic situation as other people that this exchange of being takes place.

> We must assume . . . that some real process in one person's life situation is sensitive and corresponds to some real process in another person's life situation, and that there are numerous degrees, positive and negative, of these interpersonal sensitivities.
>
> (Moreno 1937, quoted in Fox 1987: 27)

The structure of the group allows communication at a level deeper than conscious thought and feeling. For human beings togetherness is at the heart of things, not an optional extra or the by-product of the instinctual pleasure principle. Group experience constitutes its own unique kind of purposeful action, the creating of meaning from confusion, community from individual isolation. This is not simply wisdom *in* the group, but the wisdom *of* the group; knowledge that the group bestows and each member receives personally, as a gift from elsewhere. One which is able to give us 'wings'.

'Something that rises up in me . . . that I've learned to trust.' Rogers is not as explicit as Moreno, or as systematic as Tuckman or Bion. His usual concern was always with counselling and psychotherapy on a one-to-one basis. When, later on in life, he turned his attention to group methods he summarised his ideas about the stages of intensive group experience in 'The Process of the Basic Encounter Group', a paper published in 1967. This is intended 'as a naturalistic, observational picture'. It gives a blow-by-blow account of what it actually feels like to be personally involved in an experiential group. Group experience, says Rogers, makes individual awareness ever more personal; as

> The expression of self by some members of the group has made it very clear that a deeper and more basic encounter is *possible*, and the group appears to strive instinctively and unconsciously towards this goal. . . . Group members move toward becoming more spontaneous, flexible, closely related to their feelings, open to their experience, and closer and more expressively intimate in their interpersonal relationships.
>
> (Rogers 1967)

Like Moreno, Rogers lays stress on *spontaneity*, both of individuals within the group and of the group itself. Indeed, groups actually resist attempts to plan their progress in advance. 'The group will *move* – of this I am confident – but it would be presumptuous to think that I can or should *direct* that movement towards a *specific* goal' (1970: 45). In other words, a group possesses its own kind of life, and this is to be trusted and believed in, not tamed or directed – or interpreted in terms of conscious, intellectual definition.

Rogers calls this quality of life 'presence'. By this, he means an individual's awareness of other people's experience as an enabling factor within the group as a whole, the source of a new kind of life which is not to be lived or enjoyed apart from this particular gathering of persons, a kind of communion of selves which is not only consciously felt but registered and understood at a level which remains unconscious. For Rogers, presence is perhaps even more important than process. It is the group's own *wisdom* 'the wisdom of the organism, exhibited at every level from cell to group' (1970: 44).

Safety and danger

Experiencing security within the group structure.

A personal relationship is one in which individuals are related as persons, not as complementary functions in an organic process, still less as the instrument and its employer, as in the case of master and servant. (Macmurray 1933: 155)

Because their meanings emerge inductively from a holism rather than being deduced as a sum of parts, groups are kinetic icons of human relationship. There is always movement within a group, a kind of toing and froing amongst its members; that is why I say they are kinetic. Sometimes the movement is embodied, sometimes it is invisible, a kind of spiritual interchange of personhood. Sometimes, often, it is both. It is iconic because this movement expresses a spiritual reality – between, among, around, through, across, beyond – revealing itself in ways that are aural, visible, tactile, multisensorial, bringing home the two interdependent realities we call presence and absence, distance and contact. The group embodies what is mine, what belongs to you, and what is shared between us. This sharedness is a distinct category – that which holds us together while defining us as ourselves – so that the group itself is the indispensable context of particular actions of sharing, and consequently a reality which is both actual and spiritual.

As I write this I have a mental image of a group of boys, ages ranging from seven to fifteen years, standing in a circle, each of them holding onto the circumference of an open parachute. I see them considering all the things that they can and will do with this marvellous expanse of white nylon, but most of all I am aware of the parachute itself and all that it stands for, all that it *allows* in the way of shared possibility and between-ness. The parachute symbolises the tension identifying all genuine groups, the apartness which permits them to hold together. This isn't an invention but an actual memory; one that transformed my experience of groups, not only ones I participated in afterwards but all the real groups I had ever known in my life. If the group is an icon of relationship, the children's parachute is an icon of the group itself, wherever it may take place, whoever is involved.

As Martin Buber (1966) brings home so unforgettably, the mutuality which creates between-ness depends upon separation. A person cannot be in relation with someone else either by being a part of them or making them a part of themselves; and no one can be a person unless he or she is in relation. Being a person is recognising the distance that exists between you and them, and reaching out to them across it. We act as persons when we intend to make contact with the other while respecting and preserving its otherness.

To put this in another way. There is something in our awareness of being 'together' which is always there and usually overlooked, in the sense of being taken for granted. It is there even when there are only two people involved, as a presence we may either recognise or choose to neglect. It is, of course, what we call 'togetherness', the primary contextual phenomenon, the ground or context of relationship, the space in which we move with regard to each other. If we set out to analyse our awareness of our own personhood we must include this in the data available; and when we meet in groups with the intention of exploring what it is like to be human, it is this 'being separate/being together' phenomenon which provides us with most of our material.

In a group, self-identity is brought home by the concentration of other identities – other presences – which the group represents, not as an undifferentiated whole, but as an obvious interplay of relationships; not simply 'you and I' but *you-and-I-ness* present everywhere within the framework of the group. This presence holds us together as a unity. It is not any kind of outside force imposing an unwelcome conformity on us. On the contrary it springs to life among us as a vivid sense of enlarged possibilities, ways of being ourselves which are difficult to resist. Sustained by this we relax, abandoning our usual defensiveness, showing signs of ourselves that we normally keep under wraps.

Suddenly it seems worth our while to be vulnerable.

rb |

This is one reason for the regressive behaviour psychoanalytic theory associated with groups (Bion 1961). The feeling of relief and release afforded by the opportunity to relax our inhibitions 'in the safety of the group' allows us to escape from emotional pressures originating in the past which affect our ways of relating to the present, defusing transference by allowing us to form alliances of a supportive kind. At the same time, this emotional freedom makes it possible for negative feelings to be shared among members of the group, instead of focused upon one single person. When all such feelings are projected upon a particular group member, however, the effect on her or him is devastating.

Groups may seem friendly enough on the surface. It has to be remembered, however, that this veneer of civilisation may be uncomfortably thin. This is particularly true of therapeutic groups. The release of inhibitions which comes from a sense of belonging among people who are willing to confess to being, like oneself, under a painful degree of psychological pressure represents the temporary relinquishing of psychological defences. Suddenly, instead of feeling happy and safe, secure in the presence of like-minded people, a group member may feel emotionally naked, painfully vulnerable with no one to turn to – except, of course, the group leader, who may have shown every sign of refusing to become involved in whatever it is that is currently going on within the group so that they can 'work it all out for themselves'. (I have had extensive experience of membership of therapeutic groups and I know that this is true!) Other kinds of group approach take special precautions against this kind of 'scapegoat effect', dramatherapy being a case in point.

At a basic level, though, the experience of sharing one's thoughts and feelings with a whole group of other people can be a scary business. It leaves one open to all kinds of anxieties about whether or not one's own ideas and impulses will be taken on board as acceptable, so that the implicit standards, which are sensed as present in every social group, may not be offended against. This kind of 'group expectation' is always something that group members have to take account of, and there will almost certainly be times when it may appear to be extremely important, characterising people's experience in ways which are restrictive rather than enabling.

At the same time, it is this awareness of the reality of other people's presence which is the primary healing element in group therapy. Groups mediate the otherness of other people in ways that permit contact by avoiding both rejection and engulfment. They do this by creating an environment which allows a special kind of interpersonal balance, one where the risk involved in being open towards someone else is rewarded by the sense of personal validation gained from the openness of their response towards us. So we receive blessing, exchanging gifts of friendship and understanding which have been bought at the price of real personal involvement.

This exchange of challenge and reassurance is at the very heart of any kind of healing through group experience. Groups are designed to create the kind of safety which encourages people to leave their self-protective isolation and join in the common purpose of working to build group cohesion. 'I surprised myself as well as everybody else. I never thought I'd have the courage – but I suddenly felt it was OK, that I was safe among friends, so I went ahead.'

It isn't always as easy as this, of course. The achievement of a cathartic balance between danger and safety can have many false starts. It is something which we seem to have to 'learn the hard way'. The presence of other people has a tendency to put us on the defensive. We need to be reassured in ways which will carry weight for us. Words are not enough; we have to find out for ourselves, and learn to trust the group even when some members betray the trust we have in the underlying mutuality of the group's underlying intention.

What then is the group's intention? What are the assumptions a group makes about itself which make it into 'a group'? Perhaps it is easier to answer this question in the case of groups formed to bring about particular purposes – work-orientated groups in which the members share their own individual skills and experience in order to arrive at a solution to a particular problem; therapeutic groups in which the problems are more personal and their nature less easily grasped by the group as a whole; religious groups, perhaps the simplest and most straightforward of all, meeting together simply to celebrate and remember, or to contemplate a truth acknowledged by everybody present. These and other kinds of groups conform to a single purpose: they are structures for sharing. What is shared in groups concerned with exploring human personhood is not the expertise or experience of its members but their vulnerability.

These are groups concerned with promoting psychological and spiritual openness. In order to function as specifically therapeutic they depend upon a unique quality of interpersonal sharing. This may be called cathartic sharing. In other words, it depends upon the special kind of psychological reaction that gives rise to a powerful sense of emotional liberation concerning the way we are towards other people; the barriers that I have erected between myself and the people around me are suddenly removed and I reach out and touch the life that is not me and yet calls out to me in a way I can no longer withstand. I find release from my unacknowledged yearning for mutuality (c.f. Rose 2002).

At the same time, the conditions must be right for such a thing to happen. I cannot just decide that it would be an enjoyable thing to do. For one thing, this is not the kind of enjoyment I have trained myself to seek out in life. Quite the opposite in fact. Powerful emotions of a personal kind may sometimes be unavoidable, but generally speaking I don't go looking for trouble; I would mistrust anybody who did. Only under very special circumstances would I feel it safe to drop my social mask and allow people to see how upset I am. By 'people' I mean myself as well as them, and particularly myself in my personal involvement with them. Alienating feelings like anger, disgust, the need to reject what I find shocking or distasteful, I seem to be able both to display in front of others and acknowledge in myself. It is my capacity for feeling other people's emotions, for *re*suffering personal trauma as if it were mine not theirs – as in some sense of course it both was and is – that seems to embarrass me so much. The reason is obvious enough I suppose, anger, resentment, etc., afford release, the relief of drawing away from unpleasantness whereas to allow oneself to be brought into conflict with the actuality of suffering, whether one's own or someone else's is instinctively aversive, something to be shied away from and if at all possible avoided in future.

'I would like do something to help, but I'm frightened to get involved. If there was some way I could find the courage.' The need to share is strong, almost as powerful as the urge to protect oneself. We look for ways of coming to terms with other emotions apart from fear. Not to do so is experienced as a kind of self-rejection, a simple refusal to be a person at all. The organisation of therapeutic groups, like the structure of drama and theatre, aims at balancing safety and danger so that the fears which get in the way of our facing the reality of our emotions can actually be tackled 'with a little help from our friends'. In this way we work towards findings ways in which we can make sense of things about ourselves and other people which are just too painful to be thought about. Safety itself is not enough. Fear must somehow be included in the equation or we will be in danger of losing our sense of the reality of what we are trying to come to terms with – which is the danger of unprotected self-exposure.

Thomas Scheff defines catharsis as a way of discharging repressed emotions by manipulating different degrees of psychological pressure in the same way that theatre uses aesthetic distance to involve audiences by protecting them: the fact that the audience remain safely in their seats, distanced from the world of the play, gives them the courage to participate in the characters' emotions. 'Crying, shivering, laughing, etc. are cathartic to the extent that the individual is both participant in and observer of his or her own distress' (1979: 67). In other words, we recognise our own pain in that of another member of the group; seeing it distanced in this way, we can acknowledge it and the relationship we bear to it as real. Once it has been seen for what it is it can then be discharged, and even, in those cases where observation and identification balance each other, actually enjoyed. 'At exactly optimal distance, the process is not entirely unpleasant: at the balance point one is both reliving the traumatic event and therefore feeling the emotions associated with it, and at the same time observing the distressful event from the safety of the present.' (1979: 61, 67).

The spirituality groups described in this book move along 'at the speed of the slowest ship', and their content is gauged in a way that hesitates to embark on voyages of discovery that are likely to take the group itself, or any particularly vulnerable member, out of their depth. Meanings are approached at an angle, slantwise; psychologically sensitive areas are not directly probed. These groups are therapeutic in outcome not through any specifically clinical intention. Thus they manage to avoid the contra-indications for group work listed by Yalom (1970; Yalom *et al.* 1973).

Bodies speak louder than words

> Things too difficult to be talked about may be shared without using words.

The group's spiritual values are not abstract but embodied. To use the traditional theological term, they *proceed* from the actual presence of those involved. They concern the way in which a group of real people experience their relationship together, and are not to be reduced to an idea or set of ideas which the group has thought out together. There is more to group spirituality than 'brainstorming'. Everyone involved contributes to the corporate wisdom simply by being part of the group through his or her own psychophysical presence. Thus, groups preserve the holistic nature of human experience – human reality – in the face of our attempts at understanding-through-analysis. Human embodiment is an irreducible part of our shared experience; on the other hand it is far from being implied by the ways in which we think about things.

Because we are so adept at 'thinking round' the limitations belonging to having a body we tend to neglect the opportunities for personal communication that our physical presence provides us with – these do not need to be spelled out in any detail here. The first few minutes of our actual involvement within a group of our fellow human beings is enough to bring home the personal importance of tones of voice, facial expressions, gestures and hand signals, body positions – even the differences between people's shapes and sizes, ages, social positions within the wider society and in the group itself. At this ordinary, 'hands on' level we learn about one another by being together – not consciously in the sense of drawing conclusions about them, but immediately, in the moment of contact as this is brought home to us within the little world of the group. Being brought together like this is to be in a position in which we can't help making an impression on one another. We see, we speak, we touch; sometimes we pause to make sense of something said to us and work out what to say in reply, but these pauses for thought are not really detachable from the precognitive experience of actual contact with another person which gave rise to them, and from which they rebound before bouncing back into the fray. In this way we know what people mean without their actually having to tell us, picking it up in advance before returning to our own message in exactly the same way. The philosopher-scientist Merleau Ponty draws attention to the way in which our bodies pick up information about the physical environment allowing us to sense situations without actually examining them much as a motorist knows instinctively that the car he or she is driving will actually have enough space to pass an approaching vehicle even though at this distance it seems terrifyingly over-wide.

In fact, the group's context provides a vivid illustration of Merleau Ponty's conviction that human bodies possess their own bodily kind of understanding (1962). As part of physical nature they relate to their environment of things 'as to the manner born', and it is this primal congruence between human nature and the rest of creation that allows us to make our own kinds of sense out of the situations in which we find ourselves. Our kinds of sense are not necessarily identical to those that hold good in other sectors of the created universe, but because we basically fit our environment – it being the one for which we were originally intended – we at least possess the possibility of making sense, so long as we take our bodies into account as well as our minds.

The basic structure of the group, which includes our own bodies and those of our fellow group members and the actual physical and temporal circumstances which affect everything that goes on in it, makes this kind of 'contextual wisdom' stand out as extremely relevant. Human groups consist of people, not simply ideas. It is my body that earths all

my thinking, continually testing it for realism, the ability to be part of
what Martin Buber calls 'lived life'. Those ideas which immediately
influence our lives are not abstractions; or at least they do not originate
in any kind of theorising. They come from experience, and it is our
embodied experience which brings them alive for us.

Most of all, the fact of belonging together is brought home by bodies
acting as a group. Their physical presence demonstrates co-operation
without confusion. Just as bodies have the ability to receive understanding
in the most direct and immediate way, so they possess the power to
communicate it in ways that are striking and unforgettable. We sit, we
stand; we walk away and come back; we glance towards or look away
from. Our position with regard to others demonstrates an intention
towards them, a relation that exists between them and us; our feelings
about them. These are things we know by looking. We are aware of certain
aspects of whatever it is that is taking place without having to be told.
This, of course, is a basic principle of acted drama, in which people
move about in a particular setting, demonstrating their relationship to it
and the situation it creates for them by the ways in which they move in
it; using movement as a kind of language with which to communicate
among themselves what it is that is going on in this particular place and
time. The space itself represents the context of their communication. It is
what the movement is *about*. Watching this movement, in this space, we
learn from what we see (or, in the case of radio drama, what we imagine
we are seeing).

As the French playwright Antonin Artaud points out, nothing is so
eloquent as the unambiguous human gesture; and when that gesture
manages to make physical contact and becomes touch, personal worlds
are established or destroyed, for 'a touch is enough to let us know we're
not alone in the universe, even in sleep' (Rich 1978). Human touch,
human gesture, the human body itself as the instrument of a basic kind of
communication promote and encourage what Matthew Fox has called 'an
earthly spirituality' (1983: 65), rooting us in the holiness of the Creation
to which we all belong and discouraging our persistent attempts to deny
or even denigrate our embodied condition.

My mind may think well of my neighbour, intending her or him all
kinds of goodness and personal fulfilment, but it is my body which I use
to bestow blessings, whether these are visible or invisible. As bride and
groom say in the Wedding Service 'With this ring I thee wed: With my
body I thee worship' and they underline the pledge they are making with
gestures and bodily dispositions which realise their intentions towards
one another in a way that is totally beyond the capability of the words

alone. As Fox says 'To make contact with wisdom is to go beyond human words, which have, after all, existed for only about four million years' (1983: 37). The action of proclaiming love between living beings goes back considerably further – to Creation itself, in fact.

Within our culture the bodily expression of feelings is hedged about with all sorts of social regulations, so that even extremely positive impulses of affection or sympathy must be handled with discretion. Therapeutic groups, however, set out to create an environment which is more sympathetic to spontaneity and self-disclosure. Group members are encouraged to feel safer within the group setting than they do in other social gatherings, and this sense of security, of being in a place where they can at last 'afford to be themselves' exposes them to the possibility – or even likelihood – that sooner or later they will cause offence to one or other fellow members of the group and be instantly shamed into retreating into the shelter of the old defensive position, which now seems more welcoming than ever before.

The following is an extract from the diary kept by a group member.

> I'd been sitting there for a long time without saying anything. Not wanting to say anything. Not daring to. I suppose I was listening to what people were saying, but not very hard. Then something Clodagh said caught my attention: I've been there, I thought. What Clodagh's talking about happened to me, I've been there too. I wasn't going to say anything, but I began to get the feeling that people didn't really know what she was talking about. Not really, like I did. So I couldn't stop myself – I had to let her know I knew what she was talking about. I said, 'I know what you mean. Something just like that happened to me once.' She just stared at me. Then she turned away. I thought to myself, you've done it again. You've blown it.
>
> At the end of the session we all said goodbye and gave everybody gifts to take away. Clodagh gave me a piece of paper, folded over. Inside she'd written 'Thanks', and put a kiss after it.

Under such circumstances the need to reassure and reaffirm people is constantly present. Reassurance must be communicated in ways that are unambiguous and immediately acceptable. Words may be misconstrued in a way that gestures cannot. Thus, the giving and receiving of all kinds of implicit actions of blessing (verbally implicit that is, their actual meaning is explicit enough!) is a common practice in group therapy. People reaffirm one another by exchanging tokens of love and appreciation in a whole range of ways, some involving actual physical contact, some not. A favourite kind of blessing behaviour concentrates upon the giving and receiving of gifts, specially chosen by the donors in order to increase the feeling of self-worth in those to whom they are given. Under such circumstances, even the most concrete and prosaic offering gains spiritual resonance.

Only a story

> Groups create their own corporate history from the narrative of their shared life as a group.

Groups are safe meeting places for vulnerable people – safe enough to encounter one another and whatever we sense to be beckoning us from beyond. Whatever is the Other. Because group sessions possess a certain structure, in so far as they are defined by having a recognisable beginning and ending, and a space dedicated to whatever will take place between these two points, they belong to that class of human experience which is able to stand out from the ongoing movement of time as a recognisable event – an occasion, in fact. Rites of passage, ceremonial ways of marking particular stages in the lifetime of individuals or communities, possess the same basic intention as a therapeutic group. Such rituals are dictated by the need to create space for making real life changes, important shifts in the direction in which life is felt and understood to be going. There is absolutely no doubt that changes of this kind need space. They cannot be allowed to remain simply ideas. Somehow they have to become actual events. In other words they must leave the mode of thought and enter the world of action – the things that happen between people.

One way in which ideas may express themselves as actual events is within the realm of story. This is a comparatively safe way of 'trying life out for size' before embarking on actual behaviour within the real world of people and things, but this does not detract from its vital importance as a lead-in to such behaviour. As we have seen, safety is one of the two elements to be taken into consideration when we are dealing with meetings between and among people. We need to feel secure enough to reach out towards the other person in the knowledge that we may actually be rebuffed. The second element is more positive. It is the need to celebrate life. To promote joy by opening ourselves out to God and other people. It is a responsive movement and a very powerful one, which is why we may feel the need to resist it, believing that if we surrender to its force it may take us over, swallowing us up and depriving us of our precious autonomy, our right to make up our own minds about ourselves. If we give ourselves to what we most want, most need, we may find ourselves destroyed by it. Who will it leave us being?

This, then, is what the spiritual quest is actually about, coming to terms with fear. Vulnerable people, who have been wounded by life, by the quest for personal (i.e. spiritual) fulfilment know this best. Life is bringing it home to them. A psychologist might say that their psychological defences are not proving adequate to the task of protecting them from emotional challenges that they find intolerable. We all have such defences, theirs are simply not doing the job that they were designed for, and so their underlying vulnerability is beginning to show. The cruelty of life is getting through to them, in fact, and this is why they are coming forward for help wherever it may be offered.

Many of those who seek psychotherapy may be willing to accept this as a fair description of what is happening to them. Not everyone, however; some feel that to put it like this is to get the balance wrong in an important way.

> I can't say that what is happening to me is pleasant. A lot of the time it is terrifying. When I can't do the things I used to do so easily, when catching a bus or getting in the car to take the kids to school is a mammoth task I have such a sense of failure. Failure and futility. I sat down last week and made myself have the courage to walk along to the supermarket, which is two streets away. I managed to get as far as the corner by the post office, well I didn't really get that far even – I saw the corner coming up ahead, calling me on, and I couldn't manage it. I just couldn't get myself round it. I turned round and went back home. As I went I remember thinking to myself, one day I'll get round that corner and that got me thinking in terms of corners, ones that I'd really like to get round.

This is an extract from a group member's own story about herself, and it shows something about the way such stories are used. Elizabeth, the woman talking aloud about herself here is using the narrative form to say something she was not yet ready to think about in any other way. She is using the story in order to express an awareness, still exceedingly vague and fragile, that she is being called beyond herself, not simply the wounded self she feels that she is now, but the robust, capable person she used to be. She is now actually in the process of growing beyond the present into a future that will be more complete, more satisfactory than she had at any time previously imagined for herself. This is a bigger corner than those she has had to get round up to now, and she herself is weaker than she ever used to be; but her lack of ability to cope will not, in the event, stand in her way; somehow or other it will actually prove an asset.

In the meantime, Elizabeth is using her story as a way of getting round – beginning to get round – this corner. Stories may be used in an explicitly religious way to provide a narrative framework for religious teachings – as when a particular life history is used as a way of inspiring devotion and strengthening discipleship. The essential spirituality of story, however, subsists in its nature as an art form, a way of making adventures into the unknown seem safe enough to be embarked upon. Stories are spiritual because they encourage the meeting of persons by providing circumstances in which we are willing to show ourselves to one another as we are and would like to be. Although this takes place through an action of imaginative sharing, its effects turn out to be real.

This is because we make use of human reality in order to live out our imagination in corporate rituals and dramas in which people, places and times are all equally real, equally concrete. The 'place of sharing' and the 'space for change' are not simply ideas but actual locations made use of to produce the living symbolism of human relatedness, the experience of individual personhood without which there can be no reaching across, no sharing of life. Herein lies the significance of the human body and the human group to express realities that are both temporal and transcendent. Life 'within the symbol' reveals the ultimate truth which gives meaning to our existence. This is the spirituality that the group both participates in and embodies within itself. The shape of story gives life itself a symbolic dimension; the action of taking part in the structure of story provides safety for encounters that happen within it.

Ways of working together, which in the first stages of group life seemed artificial and restrictive, are humanised by the life developing among group members. Thus the life histories of groups shows them taking on their own corporate story, which is different from and more than the aggregate of the individual narratives contained within it. This shared myth making gives shape and content to people's spiritual lives as, in Martin Buber's words, '"It" becomes "Thou", inspiring and blessing' (1966: 14).

Cosmicisation

> What is felt to be true within the group becomes the symbol of a wider truth.

Characteristically, the group meets in a circle. This itself is symbolic of Cosmos and resonates with spiritual awareness of creation. Matthew Fox, writing about 'Creation Spirituality' has collated testimony from a range of world religions that 'All things are inter-related because all things are microcosms of a macrocosm' (1983: 69). When the life of a group begins to penetrate all its members it flows freely, binding individuals together so that everybody participates in its freeness and life 'It is all a blessing, an ongoing fertile blessing, with a holy salvific history of about twenty billion years' (ibid.). This is strikingly illustrated by the games people play in groups. The games are invariably arranged so that their organising principle is circulatory; the movements involved are repetitive and interactive, and players move in and out among one another in a succession of variations on a human 'chain of being' reproducing the patterns associated with the idea of cosmic healing 'and it is all in motion, it is all en route, it is all moving, vibrant, dancing and full of surprises' (ibid.).

Not all group games are as lively and inventive as this, but even when people simply sit down together to exchange stories or pass things from hand to hand, or sing together, the awareness of the cosmic remains. It is an inalienable part of the significance attaching to the human body when we pay it proper attention and see it as itself: a living person rather than a biological organism. 'We were made for something cosmic and will not fit peacefully into anything much smaller' (Fox 1983: 72).

In group games, as in other expressions of the shared life of groups, the shape of the group itself helps us to make this vital connection between macro- and microcosms which, at the same time gives us confidence and excites us. It seems that even in this very ordinary, improvised setting the imagery of wholeness and perfection affects those taking part, as people find themselves touched by the creative spirit and are continually surprised by what emerges within the group.

The idea of an enlivening and transforming presence who is both the centre and *at* the centre of the circle of creation is a perennial theme of historians of religion (Eliade 1958). For example, for Christians the cosmic person is Christ who reconciles all things in heaven and upon earth, so that even though it may be only two or three people who are gathered together, he is there in the middle of them, as an axle on whom the wheel of life turns. In Hindu tradition it is Narayana-Visnu; for Buddhists it is the Cosmic Buddha. The creativity of the centre makes the circumference creative too. Certainly small groups are as creative as larger ones; there is something about the experience of being *centred* that turns us outwards towards life in a gesture of encouragement. There is a dynamism here which seems to affect non-religious people as much as it does believers.

Whether or not we perceive a personal presence at the centre we still share in the symbolism of the circle itself. If three is the perfect number, having a beginning a middle and an end, the circle is certainly the ideal figure, moving as it does in all directions while staying immobile, or moving in its own sphere alone – in all directions, yet only one direction. The religious significance of the *mandala*, as C.G. Jung pointed out, is universal (1983). The nature of the divine perfection, the ultimate wholeness, moves everything and yet remains still, in a total union of inner and outer. The 'square in the circle and circle in the square' challenges and comforts at one and the same time, calling on us to abandon our existential isolation.

> The session was about 'coming in and going out' – being born and dying – and we were standing in a circle looking inwards. The idea was for people to think of something about saying hello and goodbye to someone, and then to take it in turns to show the others, by going into the circle and saying or doing something to do with whatever they'd been thinking about. You didn't have to do this if you didn't want to and you could ask someone in the group to help you. No way, I thought. There's no way you'll get me doing that. So I just relaxed and settled down to enjoy the show. Then, suddenly, I was *there*, right in the middle of the circle. This was bad enough, but what I was actually doing was worse, even more embarrassing. I showed them what it was like when I first said hello to June. Of course, I had to show them what it was like saying goodbye, too.
>
> (A group member who had recently lost his belovéd wife in a road accident.)

According to Otto Rank (1958), Freud's former disciple, western society as a whole suffers from the neurosis of having lost touch with the cosmos. Certainly, those whose personal universes have been shattered by the death of someone dearly loved may draw reassurance and hope from the symbolism of the group's healing embrace. This bereaved husband felt safe enough to share his feelings with people who, until a few hours ago, had been complete strangers. His thoughts warned him about the danger of becoming involved; what they were really saying to him was, keep away, you may have to remember. At a more feeling level, however, his heart drew him to respond to the group's warmth towards him. He found himself trusting the group.

Trust is a matter of body and soul, it is closely linked to the way in which we see our place within the cosmos. Matthew Fox reminds us that 'There is a necessary connection between trust learned regarding our own body and our own existence – original blessing and the blessing that earthiness is – and trust of cosmos' (1983: 83). We grow into personhood in so far as we learn to trust the setting in which we find ourselves and the other people who inhabit it with us. So far as our work with human groups is concerned, the building of trust is a primary concern and an on-going task for everyone present.

The word most often used for 'faith' in the New Testament is *pisteuein*. This actually means 'trust'. 'Your faith has healed you' may thus be translated as 'Your trust in God, the source of your life, has given you life.' Building trust within the group is a primary purpose of all group work, whether or not the spiritual significance of such activity is actually recognised. The group process described here was designed to allow members to find out for themselves the quality of the support a group is willing to give. It was not devised in order to illustrate a specifically religious idea about 'love casting out fear', although it certainly seems to do this very dramatically.

Nor was it thought up as any kind of test, either of courage or skill. An important part of the spirituality of group work is the acceptance of imperfection. At its most basic level this is Carl Rogers's 'positive regard' (1967: 53), the state of mind which refuses to entertain the impulse to feel morally superior to somebody else. This is a degree of acceptance that non-professionals (and often professionals too) find beyond their grasp, and even those who are sure they can manage it may well be deceiving themselves at least some of the time. The specifically work-shop application, however, is more practical. It is best expressed in G.K. Chesterton's dictum 'If a thing is worth doing, it is worth doing badly.'

Workshops make most of us anxious, at least to begin with. We know that we are going to be required to take part in an active way, which may involve having to do things in front of other people. The all too familiar element of competition takes over. In practice this means our choice of behaviour is severely limited; we either refuse to do whatever it is that is being suggested, or we try as hard as we possibly can to do it better than anyone else. The workshop approach sets out to avoid this kind of situation. Workshops must be designed to allow the people taking part in them to escape from the competitiveness trap by finding out their own personal ways of doing things, so that the element of individuality is recognised as more important than the degree of skill. Very early in the session people start forgetting to worry about whether they are looking clever or stupid.

In practice, timid and unsure people tend to work rather more creatively than skilful and confident ones. For a group member, skill consists in the ability to give other people confidence so that they can share in what Adler recognised as the courage belonging to imperfection (1980: 49–70). This is the ability to trust creation which lets us value other people's contributions as part of a vocation that can be genuinely shared. As Matthew Fox says 'It is shared weakness and need that draws from a group its gifts and powers of healing' (1983: 111).

The group possesses its own spirituality. It is not simply a number of spiritually aware people who meet together, or a seminar organised for the discussion of a particularly fascinating aspect of life, although it may of course take either or both of these forms, or any number of others including that of an experiential workshop whose aim is exploration rather than instruction. This latter option is most likely to take account of the actual phenomenon of group spirituality, the spirituality possessed by groups simply by virtue of being themselves. Spirituality in groups starts off with the advantage of the predisposing factors glanced at in this chapter. The people involved in these workshops had the following in common: they all started off with the same advantage – that of working within a setting that is particularly sympathetic to the study of human spiritual awareness.

Group-building workshops

These workshops are intended to serve as examples of a particular way of working, and not as blueprints to be slavishly copied. Each workshop emerged from a different set of circumstances and was designed to meet the requirements of a particular group of people coming together at a particular time and place. There is a good deal of scope for varieties of approach, so long as a few fundamental ground rules are observed. Apart from preserving the threefold shape of the structure upon which its ability to symbolise personal change depends, special attention should always be paid to

1   assuring group members of the confidential nature of everything that happens during the workshop

2   calming any fears they may have that self-disclosure will expose them to ridicule

3   establishing the fact that no one under any circumstances is to be allowed to be, or feel, victimised by anybody else, or by anything that may happen during the workshop.

If anybody wants to drop out at any time they certainly can do so – and rejoin if and when they want to. If the whole group decides it would rather not do something that has been suggested, but wants to do something else instead, they are entirely free to do so (this rarely happens, but when it does it can turn out to be the most exciting thing of all!). The leader goes along with the group, making suggestions but not enforcing obedience. When people show signs of being upset in any way the action of the workshop stops, so that the emergency can be dealt with. Regrouping only happens when everyone present feels able to proceed.

The workshops were designed to be in three parts.

1   A beginning section aimed at reducing tensions and encouraging people to enjoy the experience of being together. It involves a game or a group exercise which is both interesting and funny, but is always highly structured, so that those involved have to concentrate and there is opportunity to help one another out as a group.

2   A middle section which is more reflective and less rigidly prescribed, and sharing is of a more personal nature involving feelings which might not be revealed except among friends and 'people one can trust'. This part of the workshop will explore a theme or enact a story, using the 'group space' prepared in the first part to go deeper into pain and joy than it is usually safe to do in the presence of others.

3   A final closing section, in which the world outside the group is gently re-introduced. Group members talk about what has been happening during the workshop from the position of people looking back on something which has now finished and drawing conclusions about it.

A basic introductory workshop would be something like this.

1   Exploring the space provided, exchanging names with the group and/or finding someone to say how you feel about being involved in a group like this.

2   Finding a way to show the rest of the group what you and your partner have come up with and/or joining with everyone else as a group to portray what being a group feels like at this early stage.

3   Leaving your new group identity by 'stepping out of the circle' and saying goodbye ('de-roling').

The following workshops have taken place in various places over the last five years, with different groups, including members of varying ages and backgrounds, and both sexes.

About workshops

1
   a   Say hello to people. Who is local? Who has come a long way to be here?

   b   Stand in the part of the room which corresponds to the distance you have travelled (taking the centre of the room as your destination).

   c   Play a game in which people take turns to show how their journey was (this can be as absurd and far-fetched as they want to make it).

   d   Form into a circle and take turns to say what your name is. Try to remember people's names so that you can name everyone else (don't worry if you can't, they will help you by saying their name again!).

2
   a   Find a partner and talk to them. Does being here make you feel anxious? What's it all going to be about?

   b   Join up with another couple. Now take turns to tell the other three what being in the workshop reminds you of – memories, fears, expectations, hopes (you don't have to say anything if you'd rather just listen).

   c   Come back into the circle. Can you think of a way of presenting the feelings and ideas you have been sharing? Try to do this without actually using words. You can stand or walk in an expressive way, or 'borrow' someone else and put them in a pose suggesting how you yourself feel. Alternatively, you can use the paper, pins, finger paints, modelling clay to transmit your reactions to the rest of the group.

3
   a   Sit down in the circle. Take this opportunity to ask the group

leader any questions you may have about working in groups and to tell him/her something about how you have felt during this one.

b   Say goodbye to everybody and particularly to the three people you have been working with.

About trust

1

a   Move round the room saying hello to one another. Repeat this twice, the first time trying to be as formal as you can, the second time as relaxed and friendly as possible.

b   Listen to the music and begin to move in time to it. Try to be as relaxed about it as you can and not to bother about whether you think you're a good dancer or not! When the gong strikes, start to dance in a formal way, until you hear it strike again, when you can relax again. Go on doing this as long as the music lasts.

c   Form a circle to play the game 'still pond'. The leader allows her/himself to be blindfolded and takes up a position in the centre of the circle. The others walk around anywhere they like until the leader shouts 'still pond!' whereupon they must stand completely still. Now it is the leader's task to identify someone in the group, moving from person to person until he/she manages to do this. Then she/he exchanges roles with the person identified, tying the blindfold round their eyes and guiding them into the centre of the room. And so the game goes on, with the blindfolded person shouting 'still pond!' and everybody freezes.

2

a   Take up a position facing your partner, as if you were standing looking at yourself in a full-length mirror. Now lift your palms up so that you seem to be standing palm to palm with your mirror image. One of you slowly begins to move her/his hands and the other follows, mirroring every movement. Now swap over, so that the other leads. Practise going faster and slower, fast one leading then the other, handing over to your partner without stopping the motion; try moving round while you're doing this (you will find it easier if you concentrate on the other person's face instead of looking at their hands all the time).

b   Take your partner on a 'blind walk' round the room. This means taking it in turns to lead and be led. The person being led is first of all blindfolded, then he/she lays his/her hand on the other person's arm and allows him/herself to go wherever he/she is taken (before trying this make sure you promise not to let your partner bump into any obstacles on the way).

3

a   Sit next to your partner. How did you feel (a) leading, (b) being led? Stay together for a few minutes talking about this.

b   Move back into the circle. Share your experiences of the 'blind walk' with the rest of the group (you can swap roles and each person talk as if they were their partner if you want to).

c   Say goodbye to your partner and then to the whole group.

About spirituality

Workshop I: the flight of the dove

1

a   In a circle throw a ball to one another, saying what your name is as you throw it (the ball can be real or imaginary).

b   Take one of the feathers from the basket in the centre of the room. Let it take an imaginary shape in your hands until it becomes a bird. Now pass it to your neighbour.

2

a   Spend some time looking at the bird you have just received. You may talk to it or listen to what it is saying to you.

b   All together, release the birds into the centre of the circle. Join hands and watch the birds fly.

c   Find a partner and a place to sit and talk. Tell your partner what it felt like, both having the bird in your hands and then letting it go.

d   With the materials provided, paint, draw or model the thoughts and feelings you can remember having, when you had to say goodbye to something – or someone – you treasured (you don't have to be 'good at art', you'll come up with something!).

e   Put what you have drawn, painted or made in the centre of the circle.

f   Make a 'group sculpt' on the theme of 'the bird's flight'. This means that each person in the group takes up a bodily position which expresses this idea, and everyone joins up together in the middle of the circle to produce a kind of living sculpture. When the leader gives the word, move your positions so that the sculpt changes its emphasis from 'the flight *away from*' to 'the flight *towards*'.

3

a   Let go of the sculpt and turn towards the other group members. Say goodbye to them, and particularly to your own partner.

Workshop II: the dove's wandering

1

a   Say hello to everybody as informally as you can.

b   Wander round the room exploring it. Now fix your attention on something at the other side of the room and make a beeline for it. When you arrive at your destination do the same thing again – fix your eyes on something and move straight across to it. Do this several times, taking care not to let other people get in your way.

c   You are in Alice's garden (from *Through the Looking Glass*). Each time you set out in one direction you end up where you started – but if you go the opposite way it brings you where you wanted to go. Try this out and see how it feels!

2

a   Go for a walk outside the workshop building with another group member. While you are walking, tell your partner about a poem (or a book, a picture, a piece of music) that you like. If you see anything while you are out together, remember it so you can share it with the others (it can be anything that catches your eye).

b   Come back inside and stand or sit in a circle. With your partner's permission, tell the group about their poem (or whatever) and about anything that happened during your walk that you want to share.

c   With the rest of the group, invent a creation myth involving the elements – objects, people, incidents, poems, etc. – which people have brought back from their journey outside the building.

d   Use everybody in the group to dramatise the story, and when you have rehearsed it amongst yourselves, act out your own version of 'how things began'.

3

a   Sit in a circle and talk to one another about what you have been doing. Spend a moment or two just thinking it over quietly.

b   Hold hands around the circle and say goodbye.

Workshop III: in the labyrinth

1

    a   After saying hello to people, help build a circle of chairs in the middle of the room so that they face outwards and have their backs towards the centre. Leave one chair out of the circle. This is the only entrance (or exit).

    b   Play 'tube train'. To begin with everyone is standing inside the 'train'. They would like to get out and are pushing to get to the exit, moving round and round the space. When the leader shouts 'tube train', one person is allowed to get out. This person takes control until he or she decides to shout 'tube train' and someone else escapes. The game continues until only one person is left within the circle of chairs.

    c   Show sympathy for the group member left in the circle!

    d   Turn the circle of chairs inwards and widen it. Sit down on the chairs and listen to the leader as she/he reads D.H. Lawrence's poem *Snake*.

2

    a   Listen to the music and close your eyes. The leader takes you on an imaginary journey involving a series of dangers to be faced and obstacles to be overcome in order to win a very valuable prize – the 'pearl of great price'. Once this has been achieved, you are conducted back 'home' again and invited to open your eyes.

    b   With a partner, share some of the very difficult and painful life situations you have been through.

    c   Your partner is a sculptor and you are the stone or wood on which he/she is working. Let him/her make you into a statue of somebody who is going through the things you have been telling him/her about. Now reverse roles – *you* are the sculptor, they are the stone.

    d   Move into a circle outside the ring of chairs. Now adopt the position you were placed in by your partner.

3

    a   At a sign from the leader, come back into your normal pose and sit down or remain standing where you are.

    b   What do you think and feel about the things you have been doing in the workshop? Listen to what people are saying and join in if you want to.

    c   Hold hands in order to say goodbye.

Workshop IV: celebrate!

1

    a   Move briskly round the room, saying hello to people in passing. Now begin to move more slowly, taking time to look at people. Don't say anything, just smile at them as you pass. What do you remember about them?

    b   Find a place to sit by yourself. Write a word or a sentence about everybody (this is for your sake – you're not going to have to show anybody else).

    c   Form a circle involving the whole group. The leader announces that there is to be a celebration. Decide among yourselves what you will be celebrating together.

2

    a   With three or four other people, decide how your small group will contribute to the whole. Will you need to make, paint or draw things? Spend some time preparing and practising. Try to use ideas and motifs from your previous group workshops.

    b   Perform the ceremony you have all prepared.

3

    a   At the end of the ceremony, gather round an (imaginary) Christmas tree in the centre of the room. Is there anything you want to say about this workshop, or any other workshop you have been involved in with the group? If so, now is the time to say it.

    b   Take an invisible gift from the tree and give it to another member of the group. Try to think of something you feel will give them pleasure and add to their sense of personal fulfilment. Give them time to thank you for your gift.

    c   Say goodbye to everybody.

Chapter 2

The space between

I want you to think of this room as if it were a football field. It's a proper field, with two sets of goal posts, one at each end – but there's only one team, and you're all members of it. It's time to get ready for the big game. Who's going to play where? That's what the game is about. It's about choosing your position in the field. That end is your goal (pointing to one end of the room). That is the goal you are defending. The other end is your opponents' goal, the one you are attacking. You can stand still, but you have to do it in the part of the field where you think you belong. So, if you're feeling confident and on top of things, you'll be up there in the enemy's half of the field, right near their goal, the one you're attacking. If you're feeling less sure of yourself, waiting to see how things turn out, then you'll be somewhere in mid-field. If you feel unsure or really anxious, then find a place near your own goal. You have to use your own judgement about this. Only you know how you feel about yourself.

Space – not 'outer' or even 'inner' but actual *physical space* – fascinates us. We take it for granted that we must have room to move around in; but how much? Those who have laboured to create a more or less private world tend to find the close physical presence of other people threatening because it interferes with what they are trying to do. On the other hand those who feel unsure of their relationship with others, but can't see themselves apart from that relationship, are often reassured by the close physical presence of someone else. The space we need to move around in is matter for continual negotiation and re-adjustment.

Winnicott and 'potential space'

> The space occupied by the group becomes a 'transitional object'
> enabling relationship.

If we want to find out how groups handle space, its challenges and terrors,
we need to have a look, first of all, at the connection between space and
the origin of our own experiences of personal relationship.

> Now I was in the back part of the room, sitting on the floor playing
> with the toys. I said to the Piggle (whom I could not actually see):
> 'Bring teddy over here, I want to show him the toys.' She went
> immediately and brought teddy over and helped me to show him the
> toys.
>
> (Winnicott 1980: 9)

D.W. Winnicott describes the way he made space in what he was
doing – in this case his clinical practice – for a little girl, a procedure
that he believed to be fundamental to the business of healing her. Space
is seen here as movement; a way out of one thing and into something
else, a gap made for filling. It has, of course, to be a welcoming space,
a container for good things; but they don't have to be there already.
They can be put there. Space can be opportunity. For Winnicott, spaces
in things were there to be explored, not simply closed up. He saw our
ability to 'make space' as the measure of capability for living in the real
world. Thus the creation of actual physical space symbolises our ability
to explore real problems. These 'gaps for potentiality' are practical signs
of the relationship of persons both to and with one another; practical
in the ordinary sense of the word, as things you can make, use, live with,
not merely think about; although thinking about them has its uses too.

Winnicott describes the significance of the spaces that we make and
enjoy for ourselves (and include other people and things in) in terms
of his theory of 'potential space' (1971: 46, 106–110). This refers to a
category of reality representing a crucial stage in a child's developing
awareness of the relationship between outer and inner reality. This vital
discovery is centred upon the activity of play, which itself depends on
space to play in. This play space does not need to be extensive, in physical
terms, because imagination will extend it.

What it does have to be, however, is *real*; real in the sense of existing
in the world as an inhabitable place, an objectified idea. Winnicott was
to move on from here into his famous formulation of the 'transitional

object'. A transitional object is a thing that permits the emergence of that most unthinglike of human precepts, personal relationship. Looked at like this, the object itself, be it 'a bundle of wood or the corner of a blanket or eiderdown, or a word or a line, or a mannerism', is always a kind of place: 'It is the place I have set out to examine: the separation that is not a separation but is a form of union' (1971: 115). Obviously this is a very special kind of space in which the separateness of the presences involved is not destroyed and they remain presences *to each other* although held together by the space they share; contained in it but not restricted by it.

For Winnicott, then, 'space' becomes 'object', because it is the occasion of our becoming aware of another person. The experience of using space in this way sheds a particularly vivid light on the union-in-separation that is human relationship itself. Relationship comes into being in what happens between the therapist and his young client who are playing in a space in which neither will destroy or be swallowed up by, included in, or made to feel really unhappy by the other, having decided by mutual arrangement what the rules of the game they are playing should be. It is a game in which the expression of feelings is permitted or even encouraged, but no one gets hurt. Elsewhere they might be injured, even destroyed by such goings on, but not here; here people and things can be both present and absent. Most important of all, they can be both attacked and preserved at the same time. The game itself is an expression of love, but the things played at are sometimes not loving at all.

He suggests that this kind of game playing is so powerful and so enjoyable that it affects the way we construe whatever happens to us under the normal circumstances of life. At some level of consciousness, we remember what it was like 'in the back of the room', where concrete reality and fantasised experience were equally true, equally salient; where we were free simply to be, established as human by the confirming presence of somebody else, someone who quite literally occupied the same space and enjoyed the same freedom as ourselves. It was precisely in this experience, says Winnicott, that our understanding of relationship was first conceived – in 'the separation that is really a form of union' (1971: 115). Winnicott saw this kind of space – space 'between' – as vulnerable, easily invaded and destroyed. Much distress and actual psychological pathology was, he maintained, the result of not having known this space. Because of parenting that was either neglectful or over invasive, or vacillated disturbingly between the two extremes, the grieving child was psychologically wounded at an early stage of her or his development by being deprived of the space in which to form real relationships with other people.

In relational space, it is safe to leave the security of the known, of the self, and re-voyage out towards the unknown other. Object relations theory, founded in this practice, regards ways of being a person that are at present too frightening to undertake in 'real life'. Because the inhabitants of provisional space are encountered within the sphere of embodied or concretised imagination – because it happens 'as if' – they represent a fundamental fact about human awareness: the ability to believe two contradictory things at once, so that both concrete reality and fantasy, literal statements and the life of the imagination are equally true, equally *real* 'an intermediate area of experience that is not challenged', the epistemological authenticity of religion and art (Winnicott 1971: 13).

Therapeutic space – experience and image

> There is individuality and fusion within the group, and this promotes relationship and healing.

Basically, Winnicott is not dealing with ideas but actual experiences. What happens in the 'play room' is real because this space is a real place, somewhere that people inhabit. 'The point of it is not so much its symbolic value as its actuality' (1971: 6). Perhaps, using Winnicott as a starting point, we can make some suggestions as to what an ideally therapeutic space would be like, based on two outstanding characteristics of the actual experience of being in such a position: *support* and *freedom*. By doing this we will be a little nearer to understanding how groups work and recognising the spiritual nature of the interpersonal mechanisms which hold them together. (In order to bring home something of what transitional space feels like I have used the first person.)

Support This is a place where I can express myself. I can do this even if it involves infringing upon other people's sense of order, the extent of my freedom to express myself already having been negotiated. (A wooden plaque on a bedroom door proclaims the fact that 'This Mess Makes My Mum Mad'.) Because I am supported here in *being myself*, so that I feel myself drawing self-ness from being here, I can take chances here I could not do anywhere else. If the idea of 'letting myself go' terrifies me because it seems to mean total abandonment to forces I cannot control, whether these are within myself or outside (or both), somehow this special space seems to make it less alarming. Here, the idea of falling apart doesn't seem quite so devastating, quite so irrevocable. So long as I do it in terms of this space, I can make and unmake my own chaos, a privilege which does not obtain in other places. In other words, as I relax and reassert the way I organise my world, I can practise being myself. I can be without anxiety as I play at being, enjoying the facilities provided by a place specially appointed for activities of this kind. Because I feel supported in myself I can lose myself in whatever engages me, not in obedience to outside pressures but simply because I am engaged by it; and when I want to withdraw, to remember and speculate, there is absolutely nothing to stop me doing this too. In other words this space provides me with security to encounter its contents freely and spontaneously, so that I may invent and re-invent myself in relation to what is not me but is still my concern in being.[1]

Such is the ideal which to some extent inspires and sustains the actual conditions which any therapist can provide for his clients; and in fact there is a danger that, taken to these lengths, clients might feel abandoned by the therapist and be more distressed than ever. The model of therapeutic freedom, however, depends on a balance of freedom and control which would prevent this from happening. Support leads to freedom in the sense of being delivered from existential constraints which apply elsewhere.

Freedom   This is the experience whereby I am set free from restrictions on personal freedom that exert pressure on me in other life settings. In the therapeutic space I may experience freedom from the crowding of purposes, intentions and needs, my own and other people's, so that, defended against the demands of the environment, I can relax into a different way of being myself. One way of putting this would be to say that it is possible to feel oneself delivered both from *stasis* – the

---

1   This ideal balance represents the experience described so eloquently by Martin Buber, whose paradigm of 'I–Thou/I–It' enshrines a way of meeting another person that consists precisely in *not* attempting to get too close to them; certainly not to dominate their behaviour or invade their privacy. Contact ('Thou') and observation ('It') alternate in those relationships we have with other people that allow them to be genuinely themselves; and in fact, our own selfhood depends on our allowing this to happen (1966). Like Winnicott, Buber reminds us that human truth abides in between-ness. In the group we find ourselves supported in and as ourselves so that we no longer need to cling either to someone else or ourselves.

inability to move freely, to choose one's own way of acting and reacting, and more importantly one's own view of oneself – and *process*, in which we feel we are carried along and included in purposes not of our making and experienced as completely outside our control. In the group therapy setting, which provides me with 'space to play' I feel free to encounter the other *as* the other, and to enjoy that experience of real personal awareness that I believe to be the only genuine, authentically human contact between an individual and the world he or she lives in.

Space as language

> Understanding about relationships is transmitted in terms of the way that space is used.

The sociologist Erving Goffman has explored the ways in which we construct our social universes by carefully distinguishing the kinds of social interaction we are engaged in at a particular time 'My aim is to try to isolate some of the basic frameworks of understanding available in our society for making sense out of events' (1986: 10). These are frameworks which, while they are in use, are a dominating consideration in the way in which we interpret social life, representing the agreement to separate different kinds of reality from one another – the 'world' of business from that of the nursery school, for instance, or the army from the theatre, and to give each its own interior organisation, language, social goals, criteria for personal success or failure which will hold good in one set of circumstances but not another. What is valid currency in the Cathedral Close is rejected by the fruit machine in the pub, where it has to be turned into exactly the right kind of tokens by the barman.

All this involves the systematic manipulation of space, sometimes invisible and ideational, sometimes visible and geographical; often an idea clearly expressed in geographical or spatial terms. You could say that in so far as we have a general system for organising personal relationship throughout the world, this overall system consists in the manipulation of social space. Some cultures and social systems make more intricate and sophisticated use of it than others (there is, for instance, a lot of difference between the Japanese culture and that of the Greenland Ainu). But everywhere the principle of the 'ring-fencing' of social expectation holds good, because of the psychological need to express both distance and sameness, and to demonstrate the particular kind of individuality that comes from belonging to a group possessing an identity both *within* society as a whole and also separate from it.

Perhaps this is the most important thing about the *idea* of social space: its functional ambiguity. Space includes and excludes at the same time. It 'looks both ways'. It is this Janus-like quality that gives it the symbolic identity we use in liturgy and theatre to express and allow relationship. In my own thinking I associate dramatic space with a particularly vivid memory I have of an incident which occurred at a Moscow railway station. Joan Littlewood's Theatre Workshop Company were leaving Russia on their way back to England. The station platform was crowded with people saying goodbye. Suddenly a man in soldier's uniform pushed his way through the crowd. He announced that he was 'Champion Dancer of the Red Army' and that he intended to dance for us; whereupon he spread his arms out, bent his knees, and moving in a circle, pushing against the bodies, arms and legs that pushed in on him, cleared himself a space. Space *created* both dancer and audience; without it they were a crowd and a soldier. By quarrying an amphitheatre, he had completely transformed the relationship.

Space is about relationship simply because it concerns between-ness. It divides and unites, bringing things together and keeping them apart. Because we depend on being together and apart, individual and corporate, *in* ourselves and *for* others, and because these things depend on space – so that space is not only where we live as bodies but how we live as souls – the quality of our relational space is vital to our existence as people. Too little and we are engulfed and lose our individuality. Too much and we are isolated and lose our terms of reference as people.

Drama and ritual are both ways of exploring this vital engulfment– isolation dimension in order to create a powerful symbol of relationship between oneself and someone else, whoever they may be. We have seen that what psychotherapists call therapeutic space is created to explore the relationship between their clients and themselves: other focal points for the study of whatever lies 'between man and man' are to be found in theatres, churches and all kinds of working with groups – everywhere in fact that people have set about creating the space for between-ness.

Learning to play again

> Aesthetic distance allows group members to re-discover the freedom
> of expression and the self-discipline which originally allowed them to
> develop as persons.

In the darkened opera house there can be established between two of the audience, who do not know one another, and who are listening with the same purity and with the same intensity to the music of Mozart, a relation which is scarcely perceptible and yet is one of elemental dialogue, and which has long vanished when the lights blaze up again.

(Buber 1961: 245, 246)

In this passage from *Between Man and Man*, Martin Buber draws attention to the way in which works of art provide space for 'the eternal meeting of the One with the Other' (1961: 247). He is talking here about the relationship between fellow members of a theatre audience. Elsewhere he concentrates on the significance of the actual physical distance, exaggerated in the design of theatres since the very earliest days, between the audience as a whole and the acting area set over against them. To separate actors and audience in such a way, he says, brings home 'the stern over-againstness of I and Thou'. Thus theatrical distance originates in a consciously spiritual intention 'The ancient stage . . . is thoroughly separated (from the space of the spectator) through the cultic character that dwells in it and shapes it' (1957: 66, 68). The drama itself is framed by its own nature as drama; that is, the intention to present a life-like imitation of the things that happen between and among persons when they are not 'doing drama' (and sometimes, of course, when they are!). The stage conditions simply clarify the terms of the encounter, pointing us to where the meeting of audience and characters is to take place – the separation that divides us and summons us into what Buber called 'healing through meeting' (1957: 95–97).

This between-ness of person and person, in which each reaches out to encounter the other without engulfment or isolation, has to be learned. Not only this, the capacity for it has to develop. Most psychologists are agreed that it has no place in our original way of being in the world. In our earliest months, it would be inaccurate to say that we were only aware of ourselves, because the idea of self implies, as we saw, the notion of another. However, in the first months of my life I was aware of perceiving, and what I perceived was mine. Things came and went as part of me; I made the breast come when I was hungry and depart when I was replete. It was only gradually that I became aware that what I controlled, I *tried* to control: that in fact it had a life of its own and dealt with me as much as I with it.

All this is well known and established. What is not always acknowledged is the part space played in the discovery that the world was *a* world, something that was inhabited by others and must be shared in order to be survived. Put like this, even this discovery demands space for myself. In this context, space stands for safety, a safe place for experiment. The degree of danger to be faced outside this safe area dictates the extent to which its safety is valued and protected; the extent to which it is an area specially set aside. Winnicott describes how, for a growing child 'outside' reality, the realism of presences other than the self is gradually imported into the safe area so that it too can be made safe, like a bomb that has to be deactivated. 'Potential space' allows room for changes to be made in personal reality. It is not yet actual space, because that requires an actual other. But because the changes involved are not a simple defusing of dangerous elements but a way of learning to live with them, potential space acts as an introduction to real space, leading to the ability to allow other selves to exist and to draw oneself out of one's initial preoccupation with one's own private world. In other words, to become a person. A potential world acts as a prototype for a real one: we play at being people in order to grow into personhood. As Winnicott put it 'Cultural experience begins with creative living first manifest in play' (1971: 100).

It is important to recognise the experimental nature of this kind of playing. Barriers are broken and territory gained in two crucial ways, one directly connected with and leading into the other. Potential play is liminal and leads into actual social experience because it is safe. What is being negotiated with, in this safe space, is a very real threat to the self: at least that is how it is perceived. Our reaching out to the other as a source of life is balanced with our fear of the other as capable of actually destroying us. Rollo May describes how 'all our lives we oscillate between those two fears – *life* fear is fear of living autonomously, *death* fear is fear of being totally absorbed by the other' (1975: 19, original italics).

Not only this, however, our unconscious awareness provides evidence, via psychoanalysis, of a profound fear of our own destructiveness, particularly towards those to whom we are closest. According to Melanie Klein, the roots of Œdipal jealousy run exceedingly deep, even into our first months of life (1997) and Winnicott describes how children play 'death and resurrection games' with toys and dolls in order to reassure themselves that Mother will in fact be able to survive the murderous feelings that they sometimes have towards her. Psychological events which revive or reproduce this conflict and its resolution remain throughout our lives as some of the most vivid experiences we ever have. Looking at the experience of theatrical catharsis, Thomas Scheff draws attention to the balance between safety and danger which is able to act as a healing emotional release, precisely because the nature of plays as 'play' allows us to acknowledge the fears and frustrations we have simply through being alive – and in so doing puts us in touch with feelings that may have lain dormant for years. Drama, he says, is able to circumvent barriers that were carefully constructed a long time ago – in our earliest months and years, and have been systematically strengthened since then (1979). Cox and Theilgaard make a similar claim with regard to metaphor in general, which they describe as 'the optimal balancing of imagery, emotion and thought' (1987: 137). The secret lies in balance, the 'trade-off' between safety and danger happening wherever a place has been made safe for an encounter with the unknown, whether this is a theatre, a church or a group workshop. Workshops are *particularly* safe, being specially structured as 'protected space/time, where intragroup relationships may thrive without being threatened by intergroup agression' (Schechner 1988: 104). This workshop format itself aims to preserve an equipoise of comradeship and rivalry, safety and danger.

The confidence to create, first discovered in playing, heals wounds and encourages growth. Play space is a kind of do-it-yourself clinic. It is also a social laboratory, an environment specially designed for designing other environments. Experiments in involving first playthings, then playmates, are developed, expanded and realised in systems of social organisation. According to Erikson 'The child's play is the infantile form of the human ability to deal with experience by creating model situations and to master reality by experiment and planning' (1965: 214). Clinic and social laboratory are, he says, indissolubly linked; we have confidence in our adult experimentation because of the success we once had in solving our emotional and intellectual problems by trial and error: 'In the laboratory, on the stage and on the drawing-board (the adult) relives the past and thus relieves left-over effects; in re-constructing the model situation, he redeems his failures and strengthens his hopes' (1965: 215). Any success which adults have in solving problems of social living and societal organisation reflect the valuable use they made of the space where, by themselves and with other children, they spent so many, many hours in play.

The balance of safety and danger that allows us to acknowledge what we think and feel, to know where we are, is the place where our personal life begins and to which we return from time to time for renewal and refreshment during the course of our journeying. It is both new and old, a place of beginnings and inheritances, older than playing and planning – as old as life itself. It may be considered and argued about, but it is in the immediacy of action and gesture that the space itself speaks to us;

it may be something we ourselves construct, but it reveals otherness and allows us to encounter it. Seen like this, it is both problem and solution, separation and union, question and answer, way out and way in.

Sacred space

This safe central place of restoration and out-reach is the place where we are conscious of meeting God. It is the place of assignation where 'journeys end in lovers' meeting'. To this extent it expresses a firm intention, because it is the deliberate act of clearing a space, not for God to be in, but for us to meet him in. As always, it is our own life that needs to be interrupted in this way. However much we may feel ourselves to be led and inspired by God, it is we ourselves who have to do the clearing, choose the setting, make the welcoming gesture. It is his call and his empowering, but it has to be our intention, because *intentionality* is its message and significance. Behold, Lord, thy family, gathered here before you. Thus we *set out* to draw apart from ourselves and *enter into* his presence.

This is why, from the beginning of recorded time, the place set aside for worship in religions throughout the world is located spiritually 'outside' space and time. It is a place of truth which precedes every other kind of knowing; the manifestation of the Life which creates life. It depends on nothing human for its real identity, because everything human depends on it. It is still 'the still point of the turning world', while everything outside is caught up in motion; it is whole and complete where everything else is in part or still unfinished; it is always present, when everything else is involved in looking backwards to the past or forward to the future; it is inconclusive and expansive, being timeless and original. Thus it is perceived as *central* – all worlds and universes are arranged around it, and were created from it 'As the embryo proceeds from the navel onwards, so God began to create the world from its navel onward, and from there it was spread out in different directions' (Eliade 1958: 376, 377).

Above all, it is a place of *meeting*: the mountain whose summit reaches to the skies, the ladder set between earth and heaven, the cosmic tree whose feet are embedded in the earth's foundations and whose branches pierce the clouds, the sacred city where gods and men meet and in which they walk together at 'the point of intersection of the cosmic spheres' (Eliade 1958: 377). Sacred space is all this. It is always real for 'the source of all reality and consequently of energy and life is to be found there' (ibid.).

Put like this, sacred space–time sounds more strange and esoteric than it actually is. Most people are willing to admit that this kind of thinking exists, and that some people take it very seriously. Others, however, see it quite simply as a poetic fantasy, a distortion of psychological reality or even an illness. However, for all its set-apartness, it is perpetually at hand. We are put in touch with it, welcomed into it as soon as we acknowledge it as sacred, other, set apart. From a human point of view, it lives within our 'experience of otherness'. Imagined as far away, it makes itself present here and now. As with drama, the empty space reserved for worship is a present waiting to be inhabited, an opportunity asking to be taken up; the play and the liturgy focus our hearts and minds on which is actually happening. Wherever there is space and time, drama and religious worship are available to expand and realise life by focusing our attention on what is spaceless and timeless.

The idea of focused attention leads into one final function of separated space – its *deictic* nature, or its ability to give symbolic meaning to what it contains. This is something that writers on theatre spend a long time examining and explaining. As Peter Brook remarked, it only takes one man, walking across an empty space, to provide theatre. Not only people, but animals, objects, colours, sounds, all take on a kind of universal meaning when they become the objects of our concentration by being islanded in, and underlined by, space. The empty table in the empty place is at one and the same time *a* table and *the* table; it is all that tables are, have been and could be, all that they imply or suggest. It is the seriousness of study and the relief of a welcome meal; the loneliness of imprisonment and the relaxed conviviality of a game of cards; the clamour of a public meeting and the quietness of the classroom during playtime. Because it has taken on a symbolic identity it is also the absence of all the things it stands for, as symbols always point in both directions at once, forcing our minds to contemplate the alternative of what they present, and then the alternative of the alternative, and so on.

It is this that makes the actual physical distance between auditorium and stage work. Theatrical distancing resides in the power of our *symbolic awareness*, the way we regard the things we perceive because of our attitude towards them. What they *mean* to us. This is most clearly seen in drama which is overtly religious. Karla Poewe reminds us that in religion 'intellectual surrender follows emotional surrender . . . intellectualism has very little to do with the *process* of a person's being made in the image of God' (1999: 198, 204). The worldwide experience of religious people adds irresistible weight to a view of religion as rooted in the actual experiences of life. Just as drama itself is a centring of personal existence in the action of turning to the other in order to give and receive life, so religious rituals direct our search for meaning to the source of all truth, to be understood first of all in terms of the language of the heart. Des Pres describes how in the active imagination of dramatic exploration, meaning is disclosed to us as existing 'no longer above and beyond the world; it re-enters concrete experiences, becomes immanent and invests each act and moment with urgent depth' (1977: 77).

Workshops about distance

I The island

The process of constructing a 'safe place' for self-disclosure involves that of deconstructing some of the threatening aspects of current reality. Spirituality workshops discount the force of depersonalisation in existing social rituals and the neuroses which they give rise to, and substitute a new metaphoric space for encounter. The socially contrived world which holds us fast in its grip is dramatically transcended as our maps of personal reality are opened out to the action of spirit.

The following is a brief description of a series of three spirituality workshops which were designed to explore the expertise of imagining a special kind of safe place away from the pressure and preoccupations of life in the 'real world'. The purpose here was to create conditions for reaching out to make contact with other people in ways which would allow them to 'be themselves'. In other words, the project aimed at achieving a situation of shared safety – the kind of thing that the existential psychologists refer to as a healing relationship. It took place in a large, warm, comfortably furnished room, where there was plenty of actual space to move about in, and enough privacy for the people, who were 'all in it together' (whatever 'it' turned out to be), to develop a degree of intimacy as a group. In other words, the safe-space metaphor could take on the reality of an actual time and place in which real things could happen to real people and actual personal changes could come about.

Those taking part met together at a Christian pastoral care centre in the last month of the old millennium. There were eleven people in the group including the leader, the only one professionally experienced in either liturgy or drama. The oldest group member was in her late sixties and the youngest somewhere between twenty and twenty-five years. The retreat centre is itself a place which people think of as being set apart from the busy world, somewhere they can afford to take time off to be themselves. All those present, including the group leader, were involved in a process of rediscovering a sense of self, a measure of spiritual repose prior to having to re-engage with the pressures of life 'outside'. The house itself was a zone of safety and peace focusing on the room in which the sessions were held. At the heart of this was the dramatic structure of the therapy, so that there were in fact three concentric circles of safety surrounding the various activities in which people found themselves involved; each in its own way underlining the message about emotional security. This sense of separation was complemented by two other important factors, namely the presence of the group, offering companionship and support, and the theme of the drama itself – perhaps the most important factor of all.

In this case the plot of the dramatic action had been worked out in advance by the leader. This is not the only way of doing things. Sometimes ideas about storylines emerge from the group itself, and in some ways this is the most natural and spontaneous way of doing things. On this occasion, however, the nature of the occasion pointed to a particular kind of subject matter, one suggesting the experience of becoming involved in a geographical location and timescale quite different from one's ordinary existence; which is why the leader seized on the idea of an island – preferably one at a considerable distance from the mainland, and separated from it by the kind of ocean which is subject to high winds and frequent, dangerous storms.

Session one

The leader explains that this is an introductory session. Its purpose is to give the group a chance to get used to the basic, underlying idea of using the imagination to construct a world of places, people (and other kinds of creatures) and things which can be shared. In other words, it is a session about rediscovering how to play together in a way you may not have done since you were a child. The instructions given to the leader are shown here in an abbreviated form. (In fact, she spent some time explaining what she meant. Only the gist is given here, for reasons of space.)

1   Stand in a circle. Each person catches a ball thrown to him/her by another member of the group. Before throwing it to someone else, group members say what their own names are. In this way each person learns the names of some of the others and can then say the other person's name before throwing it to him/her. (This is designed to be complicated enough for the kind of mild confusion that gives rise to laughter.)

2   Take a partner. The leader shows people how partners can mirror one another's actions by standing facing each other as if they were looking in a mirror. One person 'leads' and the other 'follows', and they take it in turns to do this. (People tend to find it easier if they concentrate on the other person's face, looking them in the eye instead of trying to work out which way their hands are moving. The purpose of the exercise is to increase awareness of the real presence of another person interacting with oneself, which is why we find ourselves being first follower, then leader, then follower again, moving backwards and forwards without ever consciously swapping roles.)

3   Stay with your partner, but find a space in the room which you can claim for yourselves as a pair. Partners take it in turns to tell each other the history of the clothes that they themselves are wearing. (For example, where I bought these shoes, who gave me this necklace, etc. You can go into as much detail as you want, but try to make it interesting because your partner's going to have to remember what you said!)

4   Return to the circle. Everybody takes turns to tell the rest of the group the story of their partner's clothes. This is done by 'reversing roles' (i.e. I take on the role of my partner and talk as if I were wearing the outfit he or she has just been telling me about).

5   Find somewhere where you feel you have some personal space. On the piece of paper provided, write or draw something that expresses something about yourself – a word, a sentence, a symbol. Do this quite quickly.

6   Fold your paper and deposit it in the part of the room that feels safest to you, or the part you like best. When you've done this, go and sit somewhere for a minute or two. Take time to reflect on what you have written or drawn.

7   Sit in a circle. The leader suggests that people close their eyes (if this seems a little frightening to anybody, it's OK for them to leave theirs open). The leader takes the group on an imaginary journey to an island many, many miles away from the room they are sitting in, the house itself and the country in which the house is situated; it involves journeying together to the harbour, taking a ship and setting sail; running into stormy weather and having to abandon ship and take to a raft; finding themselves becalmed after the storm; finally being washed up on the beach.

8   Open your eyes. You have arrived at the island. The leader explains that this is a welcoming island 'the island that loves to be visited'.

From now on, and throughout the next two sessions, this room will be *their* island. It will be a place of opportunity and peace, to be explored and enjoyed. The leader invites people to spend a few moments exploring the island/room. Is there anything they would like to take away with them to remind them of it until they come back tomorrow?

9   Say goodbye to the group, telling them what you're going to carry away with you. Then say a personal goodbye to everyone individually.

Session two

This and the following session make up the main part of the dramatherapy process. Again, they start with some time spent establishing the experience of the room as an island. Since session one, which took place yesterday evening, the group have all been to bed, got up and had breakfast. Yesterday may seem somewhat distanced from where they are this morning. They can't simply jump back twelve hours.

1   Stand in a circle. Greet everyone present by name (or ask them what their name is, if you can't remember, be sure to tell them yours).

2   Imagine you are standing on the beach. You can hear the roar of the surf in the distance. Close your eyes. Can you feel the sun on your face? Can you smell the breath of the sea in your nostrils? Try moving your feet in the sand. Shift them until you feel you're standing firm in the sunlight. Now there's a wind blowing from the sea. It's blowing really strongly, so that it makes you sway like a tree. There's a storm blowing up, so that you can feel the first drops of rain on your face and forehead. It's heavier now; can you still stand upright? (and so on, taking special care to bring people through the storm and out into fairer weather).

3   Now imagine you are either (a) a wave of the sea, or (b) a strong tree at the edge of the land. You can spend a few moments 'getting into character'. (Some may find they have to take positive action to suspend their sense of the absurd at this point.) Join forces with the other waves and trees in the group. Can the trees withstand the power of the waves or will they be swept away by the storm-driven sea? (This is more of a ballet than a battle, as people's energies are directed towards 'staying in character'. Alternatives to trees versus waves are rain versus earth, rocks versus mountain torrent, etc. It can be done to the right kind of atmospheric music.)

4   Find a partner and take a walk with them round the island. Show each other what you find there. (Don't forget you can touch, smell, feel things as well as just seeing them.) Take your time; you have twenty minutes to do this.

5   Sit in a circle on the ground. With your partner tell the others what your journey was like and what you found on the island. What sort of island is it?

The couples described the island in great detail. In a way that I can't really explain, the five island narratives seemed to resemble one another in the things described – the settlement located by two pairs of partners would turn out to be in the same corner of the island, near the same kind of beach (for instance) as the ones mentioned by two other pairs; the dangerous, unexplored parts of the island would similarly turn out to be in the same place, near the same mountain range or patch of swampy ground: 'over there's dangerous,' one person said 'but it's valuable. There's something worth having. Something precious.'

6   Still sitting in the circle. What sort of animals, birds, reptiles, fishes inhabit this island? Write the name of one of them on a small piece of paper and put it in the centre of the circle. When everyone has done this, look at all the papers and make up your mind which of these creatures most resembles the kind of person you think you are. Which of them is most like you?

7   With your partner again. Take on the character of your animal, bird, reptile, fish (or whatever kind of creature you have chosen) and tell your partner something about the way you pass your life. Then swap over so that she or he can tell you, in character, about their experiences as the creature they have chosen. When you have spent some time doing this, go and choose another creature to 'be'. This time, however, try to discover a creature who reminds you of someone else, someone you know and maybe have strong feelings about, one way or another. Go back to your partner and let your new character speak to her or him. Let *this* creature talk to your partner about you. What does it think about you? How does it feel with regard to you? Let it talk quite freely because, when it has finished speaking about you, *you* are going to have the chance to tell your partner about *it*! Everything you feel about it. So do this . . . then let your partner go through the same routine with the animal character they have chosen. Then go back to sitting in the circle.

8   Everybody sitting together in the circle. Going round the ring, people

choose one of the creatures that they would like to be and explain to the group why they have chosen this particular animal, bird, fish or reptile. (They do this without actually taking the role of the creature, for example 'I've chosen an eagle because I'd like to have that kind of freedom and strength.' In this way they de-role from the parts they have been playing and become group members again, talking to each other about the animals they have chosen and their reasons for choosing them.) The leader asks the group to imagine that everyone is sitting round a camp fire at the end of a day on the island: 'It's getting towards turning-in time. Let's say goodbye and go back to our tents.'

Session three

The second session was before lunch. This one took place in the afternoon of the same day. As with sessions one and two, session three is in three main parts – a beginning, a middle and an end, with the most psychologically testing part in the middle. At the same time, however, it forms a kind of climax to the process people have been going through during the dramatherapy.

1   Stand in a circle so that you can say hello to the group. Then take some time to greet individuals.
2   Walk round the room letting it become the island once more. Close your eyes and imagine you are walking on the beach. Move your body, kicking your feet through the dry sand; walking on sand that's too hot for comfort; running over the ridges that the waves have left behind in the sand; dabbling your toes on the edge of the sea or dipping into rock pools; exploring caves in the cliff edges, etc. Find your favourite spot on the island and spend some time enjoying it. Take someone else – perhaps another pair of partners – along to see it and enjoy it with you. If you and your partner actually built a hut or a house, show this to them and let them explore it. Relax and listen to the music.
3   Draw, paint or crayon a map with your partner, of the island as you and your partner discovered it in session two. (You are allowed half an hour to do this so you need not rush. It isn't meant to be a work of art – unless you want to make it one – simply a way of remembering the shape of the island and the position of the things on it.) Do this as a pair, without consulting any of the others.

4   Back in the circle again, show your map to the others and let them ask you questions about it. What are the other maps like? How do they differ from yours?

In fact, the five maps turned out to have much in common with one another. They were all much more rounded than angular, three of them being a shape which corresponded more or less to an amoeba (or a foetus?). All three had a semi-circular northern edge and a sandy bay scooped out of a southern coastline. The other two maps were less regularly shaped; but they also resembled each other. I don't really know why this should have happened; there certainly wasn't any overt conferring between pairs. I simply thought it was worth recording.

5   Put the maps on one side and split into two groups. Working together as a team, construct a creation myth for the island. How did the island come into being? Who created it? Did it create itself? Show how the island was created in a dance or drama you have worked out together. You'll need to do this somewhere where there is space to move about in and rehearse. If one group stays here in this room, the other can use the room next door. When you are ready, you can enact your creation ritual for the other group, using the island space we have dreamed up for your stage.

One of the rites was accompanied by a narrative commentary which held the action together. The movements of this group were focused on a still centre, so that the impression given was of a flower uncurling outwards, then contracting in on itself before spreading to its fullest extent and then clustering into separate blossoms. It was most moving when it evolved spontaneously during rehearsal. The other was more light hearted and also more dramatic, although at one point it teetered on the edge of farce, one member of the group having discovered a finger puppet inside one of the props provided by the leader. This seemed too good an opportunity to miss. The knitted mannequin was brought right into the heart of the action by being 'born' at the appropriate moment. Taken in context, this touch of the ridiculous had the effect of making the rite more human and consequently adding to its power rather than detracting from it. These rituals took up a good deal of the group's energy, emotional as well as physical. When they had finished nobody said very much; there was a feeling of having shared something valuable.

6   Sit in a circle on the ground. Take time to say anything you feel like

saying. Because we are going to say goodbye to the island for the last time you may want to think about what you intend to carry away from your life here. You may like to think of something from here you could give to somebody else in the group for them to take away with them. Imagine that the island is spread out here in the centre of the circle, as it appeared on your maps. If you walk out into the centre, you can choose something.

Somebody pointed out a place on the imaginary map where there was the remains of a camp fire in a clearing of the forest. One by one, in their own time, people walked into the clearing, stayed for a moment, and then returned bearing (imaginary) gifts. These were distributed and goodbyes were said.

II 'All in it together'

The following is a series of three workshops which took place in the open air, in a clearing at the edge of a forest. I have described them in greater detail, hoping to give an impression of the way that a feeling of freedom and spontaneity can arise among people who, in any other circumstances, would consider themselves to have little in common.

Workshop I

Including Brian and Zoë, who are leading the session, there are eight people present: Colin, Mavis, Jenny, Philip, Sandra and Pauline. Colin is a doctor, working with elderly people; Mavis is a probation officer, married to Colin; Jenny is a retired teacher whose husband died three years ago; Philip is the vicar of a nearby church, and is a bachelor; Sandra is training to be a teacher; Pauline is a computer programmer – both are unmarried; Brian has a small engineering business and Zoë is his wife. Most of the group have met one another before, but Philip and Pauline are strangers to everyone here. This is the first session and people are subdued and rather nervous. Philip covers up his nervousness (or tries to) by talking rather a lot, which has the effect of making everybody quieter than they would normally be. To begin with Brian suggests that everybody stands in a circle. He says that although some people may know some of the others, there are some who don't know anybody at all. He says that he knows a game which will help people to learn one another's names. This involves throwing and catching a ball. It starts very simply and gets harder as people have more to remember. First of all everybody throws the ball to everybody else, and when someone catches it they say their own name.

Mavis   I'm Mavis and I'm throwing this ball to you.

The next stage, when everyone has practised this for a bit, is to say your name, along with the name of the person who has thrown the ball to you.

Mavis   I'm Mavis and I've received this ball from Philip, I'm throwing it on to *you.*

In the final stage of the game everybody says the name of all three people involved in the transaction.

Mavis   I'm Mavis and I've received this ball from Philip, I'm throwing it to Zoë.

This is a good way to remember people's names, as well as being fun. It's actually even more fun if you 'forget' to bring the ball and people have to mime throwing and catching. This has a very definite advantage when there are people in the group who are not expert at catching balls, or people who like to throw them very hard!

Philip   Do you mind if I sit down? I've not laughed so much for a very long time.
Zoë   Of course not, We'll all sit down, shall we? (*They sit down in a circle, using camp stools, cushions, etc.*) Right, then, off we go. Names. I'm very lucky. I've got a splendid one. At least I think it's splendid.
Pauline   It's a bit posh.
Brian   It means 'Life', so that can't be bad, can it? What does your name mean, Pauline? Do you know? Let's go round the group, each of us saying something about our names. If we don't know what they mean, we can say something about them.
Zoë   Whether we like them or not, for example.

They all do this. Mavis says she has no idea what her name means, although she has always liked it. She is delighted when Jenny tells her it means 'song thrush'.

Mavis   I do a lot of singing.

Brian suggests that now they know a little bit about one another they might find out about the place they are sitting in.

Brian   It's full of interest, this part of the forest. They used to burn wood for charcoal here. You can see where the huts used to stand. Just walk round and see what you can find that's interesting. When I blow the whistle, stop where you are and speak to the person nearest to you. You can tell them what you've found. I'll blow it again for you to move on. Then I'll blow it a third time and you can touch someone (ask permission if you feel you need to). The fourth time I blow the whistle we all gather here again. Now off you go, don't hang about, find as many things as you can.

People start doing this with varying degrees of eagerness, Jenny showing the most interest and Pauline and Sandra the least. Pauline and Sandra would prefer to stay close to each other for mutual support. Nobody is sure what's going to happen next. After a few minutes interest begins to lag somewhat.

Brian   Let's take a break, shall we? We've got some orange juice, if anybody would like some. We'll sit down again for a few minutes.

They do this. Nobody says anything for a minute or two.

Philip   That's a lovely tree. I was looking at it. So was Jenny.
Jenny   I think it's beautiful.
Pauline We should have been further into the forest itself, not out here on the edge, if we want to look at trees.
Zoë   Perhaps we don't always need real trees. We've all got forests in our minds. Was there anything in this bit of the forest that brought back memories? Did it remind you of anywhere you remember? Or perhaps it contrasts with places you've know in the past or know now. Perhaps there's somewhere in particular, somewhere special?
Brian   Let's get as comfortable as we can and see what we can remember. If you're not comfy where you are, move around until you find the right place to sit. You can lie on one of the

big cushions. The main thing is to feel as comfy as you can. That's right, wriggle around; now try to relax.

Zoë   We've all got forests in our minds.

Brian   So close your eyes and let your mind wander. How deep is your forest?

During the pause for drinks he has put a tape on the tape recorder and turned it down as low as possible. Now he turns up the volume so that it is playing very quietly in the background. It is the slow movement of a Bruckner symphony – real woodland music. The tape plays to the end and is gradually faded out.

Zoë   (*quietly*) Did you find your forest? Was it still there? Was it as good to be in as you hoped or as frightening as you feared? Look round. Find someone to share this with.

What happens next might have been predicted. Colin and Mavis stay together, as do Pauline and Sandra. Philip and Jenny look at each other with eyebrows raised, and become the third couple.

Brian   You and your partner are going to work on those memories for a bit. So find yourselves part of the space where you won't bump into anybody else, because you may need a bit of space.

Philip   Look, I'd rather . . .

Jenny   Come on, Philip. In for a penny . . .

Zoë   You're going to have to use all of the space because you're each going to show your partner something about the forest you've been remembering. You can use some words, but not many. Simply concentrate on showing what it was like, what it felt like to be in it. How would you be feeling if you were in it now? And so on. You can say what colour and texture things were, or describe sounds and smells. Who lived there in the forest? When each of you has finished you can say a bit about your connection with this particular forest.

Brian   When you've both had a go, come back and sit down.

He and Zoë sit in the centre of the clearing and wait for the others to join them. The first to come back are Colin and his wife.

Colin   You don't expect us to say where we've been, I hope.

Mavis   What do you mean? I don't mind saying!

Colin	Oh all right then. If you'll describe mine, I'll do yours.
Brian	Hang on a bit, both of you. Let's wait 'til the others get back.

Pauline and Sandra come and sit down. They don't say anything. Jenny and Philip are taking their time and are still deep in conversation. When everyone has sat down in the circle Zoë says

Zoë	First of all, Colin and Mavis, you needn't worry. You're not going to be asked to describe the forests, neither your own nor your partner's. You're quite safe!

Both appear to be relieved at this. Pauline seems a bit disappointed by it. Jenny and Philip definitely want to talk to the others.

Zoë	I'm sorry to disappoint those who want to tell everyone what they've been doing; but this is our first session and we need to move slowly at first. There may be some who don't want to share everything with everyone else.
Brian	Getting to know one person is enough for session one.
Zoë	But you can say anything you want about what it felt like doing it. How did it make you feel? Did it make you feel sad or happy? Let's talk about that, shall we?
Mavis	Well, it certainly brought things back to me.
Colin	To both of us. It was something we both remember.
Brian	You mean, you both thought of the same place?
Colin	That's right. We go back a long way, you know.

There is an amazed pause.

Philip	No wonder you wanted to talk!
Mavis	I suppose we do share a lot of things. All the same, it was strange, wasn't it?

Everyone else seems to think so, including the leaders. There is a pause, while the others decide whether or not they want to say anything.

Jenny	(*tentatively*) Mine was quite ordinary really.
Philip	So was mine. I was moved by what Jenny showed me and what she said about it. I don't know why.
Jenny	I suppose it's one step at a time.
Zoë	Moved. That's what you said. Was anybody else moved?

Pauline   Yes.
Sandra   (*after a pause*) Yes.
Brian   One step at a time.

Soon after this the group disperses, each person saying goodbye to everyone else. They arrange to come to the next workshop.

This workshop was one way of making a 'frame for story', so that a living symbol could be shared by the group in the form of an experience rather than an idea. Zoë and Brian hoped that, as the course of workshops went on, a way of thinking and feeling would emerge which was at once formal and expressive, ordinary and poetic, immediate and symbolic of timelessness.

As the workshops continued they became slightly more self-conscious, as people began to enjoy the experience of taking the unseen seriously and using it as a way of getting closer to other people, a safe place for meeting and sharing. The forest space became a symbol for this kind of sharing, and we watched the weather reports anxiously – it wouldn't be the same if we were rained off and had to go somewhere else.

Workshop 2

The setting and cast are the same. Again, the weather was fine. The first thing to notice about this session is that there is much less tension in the air than there was at the beginning of Workshop 1. People are beginning to enjoy the approach and to discover the effect that it can have on their state of mind during the week. It is a bit more difficult to get things going today because people want to chat together about things that have happened since they last met. Then Zoë starts this week's workshop.

Zoë   Shall we find partners again? It's easier to do now, when we know each other better. So find a partner and give yourselves a bit of room. Now face each other. We did a lot of sharing last week, didn't we? So that's where we'll start off today. I want one of you to be someone looking in one of those full-length mirrors and the other to be their reflection. Mavis, Colin and Pauline are 'A's and their partners are 'B's. If you put your hands up, your mirror image almost touches you, palm to palm. See if you can put your palms so close that you can feel the warmth coming from the other person's hand – but do this without actually touching. Shall we try this?

People experiment for a few moments, trying to sense each other's warmth without actually touching. This leads into the mirroring exercise described on page 38. Pauline and Sandra start off skilfully, and the other two couples are soon moving fluently in unison. Colin and Jenny start to move across the room, Jenny taking over from Colin and leading the hand movements. Everybody is laughing.

Brian	Another minute doing this, then.
Colin	Spoil sport! So what are we going to be doing this week?
Zoë	Well, we thought we'd do something about stories this week.
Brian	What do people feel about stories?
Pauline	(*after a pause*) Some stories are true and some aren't.
Philip	That's very true. (*everybody laughs*)
Zoë	Yes, but what makes something into a story?
Philip	It's the way you tell it! (*more laughter*)
Brian	Is it only that? I mean, things can happen one after another but it doesn't make a story, does it?
Jenny	Well, it depends. It can be part of a story.
Zoë	Yes, it can go into a story.
Brian	Hang on a minute. Let's try something out. We'll work in pairs again, 'A's and 'B's. Let's see if this works. What about if 'B's invent a story and tell it by using 'A's as a kind of visual aid? 'B's think of a very simple story, a couple of minutes long, no more, about something happening to somebody, and put 'A's into a series of positions which tell what the story is. Let's have a go at this – see if we can do it?
Zoë	The first thing is for 'B's to think out their stories. Just a simple story with a beginning, a middle and an end. Something that happened to somebody, for example. You can put your partner into as many positions as you want. If you make them play different parts, you must say 'this is somebody else', otherwise try not to say anything. Just show us. When the 'B's have finished, it's the 'A's' turn.

For a few moments there is hardly any reaction at all: everybody is waiting for someone to make the first move. Couples simply stand and gaze at each other. Then almost simultaneously, they begin to get down to work. Brian and Zoë move among them, encouraging and giving advice. This goes on for about a quarter of an hour, and when everyone is more or less ready, the 'B's present their stories, one by one, to the rest of the group, followed by the 'A's. This is 'done in the round', the group forming a circle. Two of the stories are episodic adventure sagas, but each of the other four revolves around a particular incident, leading up to it and away from it with varying degrees of skill. Sandra and Pauline show the greatest narrative ability, along with optimum hilarity. When everybody has finished and people have been congratulated, Zoë asks everybody to sit down and relax, still keeping in a circle.

Brian   (*appreciatively*) Well, we've seen some pretty good stories, don't you think?

Zoë   What's the most important thing about a story, then?

Jenny   Imagination?

Colin   Shape.

Brian   What do you think, Jenny? Imagination? Shape?

Jenny   Well both, I think. But definitely shape.

Pauline   That's what we had to do. That's what makes it hard – getting the right beginning, middle and end.

Sandra   Colin's story was two stories, put together. Mine was really *three* stories.

Zoë   Shall we think about this for a bit?

Brian   Let's think of some stories. Any kind of story – fairy stories, legends, books you've read.

Zoë   Bible stories, parables, anything you want. We'll go round the circle, saying the names of stories. Don't think what you're going to say, just say the first story you think of, and we'll pause for a second and think about its shape. Has it got a beginning and an end? Does it come to a climax in the middle? We'll go round a couple of times, then we'll say goodbye to one another for this week.

Mavis   This episode, you mean.

Led by Zoë and Brian, everyone holds hands.

Philip   So let's say goodbye. I'll start – goodbye everyone.

Workshop 3

The same setting and cast. When everybody has arrived, Brian suggests that the group should formally say hello to each other.

Brian   Let's all do it as ceremonially as possible.

He goes round the group, solemnly shaking hands and enquiring as to people's health. The others do the same. People begin to giggle. Zoë suggests that they go round again: this time they should imagine that they haven't seen the other person for years and years, and are completely amazed to discover them. They do it a third time, this time expressing shyness and timidity (Jenny's suggestion).

Colin   Well, we seem to know each other by now.

Zoë   How well do we really know each other, I wonder? We try to be honest with one another – but that depends on how honest we are *with ourselves* about ourselves, doesn't it? We can't share things if we ourselves refuse to recognise their existence, can we?

Philip   I've thought of a game we could play about this.

Sandra   You mean confessing things to one another? You can count me out, for a start!

Philip   No, I don't mean big things. Anyway I think confessing big things is quite easy for some people. I mean things about ourselves we're not sure someone else would understand. If we each chose a partner and said something like 'would you think less of me if I told you, etc. etc.' it could be anything at all, but it must be something a bit hard to admit. And you don't have to tell anyone else. Just your partner.

People try this out. Sandra moves immediately towards Pauline, but finds herself intercepted by Jenny. Pauline and Colin form a second pair, and Mavis and Philip a third one. Zoë and Brian hover on the edge of things, Brian looking slightly anxious. People seem to enjoy the experience however, and after a few minutes they come back into the centre of the clearing looking considerably more cheerful than they did at the beginning of the workshop.

Zoë   Well, then. Now let's do some work with the group as a whole. We're going to make some 'sculpts'. A sculpt means that you use your bodies as if they were lumps of clay. For instance, if I wanted to do a sculpt expressing joy I'd use Brian as my raw material and mould him like this. (*she demonstrates, putting Brian into an expressively joyful pose, arms outstretched, head back, corners of mouth and eyebrows raised, etc.*) We're not going to do individual sculpts, however, we're going to do group sculpts. Everyone here is going to do a sculpt of him or herself, using everybody else as 'clay'.

Jenny How on earth are we going to do that?

Pauline It's going to take a long time, isn't it? If we use you and Brian as well it'll mean making seven statues of ourselves!

Zoë explains that there will be only one statue of each person, but it will consist of the whole group, because each one will have the opportunity to build up a living image of her- or himself using the other group members to represent different aspects of his or her character or personality.

Zoë For instance, if I were doing 'me', I could choose Pauline to stand in for me – (I'd put her here, standing like this); then I'd have Colin to represent my stubbornness (go on Colin, look stubborn and stand here by Pauline – fists up and lean back from the chest); then Sandra to be my creativity (I'm not sure how you show that: Oh yes, that's marvellous!). And so on. Use as many people as you want. Perhaps you'd like to think for a moment and look back over your life. What sort of person do you think you really are?

This interests people, but takes some time to get going, because nobody wants to take the plunge. Jenny is the first to complete her sculpt. When she has finished Zoë invites people to alter it if they think she's got it wrong in any way.

Pauline Yes, she hasn't put her kindness in. Somebody's got to be Jenny's kindness. Right in front, next to shyness!

People make this kind of adjustment to several of the sculpts, taking the opportunity to express feelings about one another that they would have found difficulty in communicating in any other way. These adjustments were all appreciative (although Pauline adds 'wicked sense of humour, worse luck' to Sandra's sculpt).

After the final sculpt, the group sit down in a circle and share their reactions. There is quite a lot of agreement that the sculpts were 'pretty nerve racking' (Colin), but people seem to feel that they have been a good way of exploring their feelings about themselves. Those who have had their sculpts adjusted in a favourable direction are particularly reassured by the experience. The group is a good deal closer and more mutually supportive.

Before leaving they stand in a circle, with their arms around one another's shoulders. They sway first to the right, then to the left, letting the circle of arms take the strain. (At this point it actually started to rain and everybody ran to take shelter under the trees until the storm had passed over, before returning to the space.) Everybody holds hands and remains silent for a few moments, enjoying the sensation of being back. Then they say goodbye to each other.

Jenny   We must come here again. It feels as if it's our own space now.

Chapter 3

Story into archetype

People in pairs, talking to their partners. They are not standing around: this isn't a party. Each individual is concerned almost exclusively with the person they are with, either listening to them or talking to them. The listener doesn't interrupt at all, but simply listens. The talkers talk to their partners, sometimes looking at them, sometimes not, but always very much aware of them. Now and again the partner replies, but not often and not for long. The couples move in one direction only, down the length of the room. Some pairs are moving faster than others. Two couples are standing quite still, one pair close to the other, each completely engrossed in their own business and oblivious of the other pair's presence.

- I don't want to talk about this bit, if you don't mind. The next thing was . . .
- Do you understand me? Do you know what I'm talking about? No, but do you understand what I'm *saying*?
- That's it. That's what it was like.
- It was the usual stuff, I suppose. I wasn't any different. I don't suppose they were either. I'm sure everybody goes through this, don't you think?
- I was OK. I had my friends. Time's a great healer.
- Well, at least I knew where I was. That was something, I suppose.

Some of the people who have reached the other end of the room are silent, some are still talking to their partner. They are waiting for other couples to arrive. This isn't a race, however. Nor is it what it most closely resembles – a mobile counselling session with as many counsellors as clients. In a moment, when everybody has arrived at the end of the room each pair will set off again, now moving in the other direction back up the room. This time, however, they will have swapped roles, so that those who were talking so much before are now concentrating on the business of listening.

- I wanted to say this before, but it wasn't my turn. When you said that about . . .
- Would you think less of me if I told you that I . . .
- I never had that you see. Never. Never.
- Thank you for telling me. I remembered, when you said. I'd forgotten. How can you forget something like that? When it happened to me . . .
- That's when my world ended. Up until then . . . (see Figure 3.1)

'Up until then', 'after that', 'all that time', 'a turning point', 'one of the landmarks', 'like coming home again'. It is a symbolic journey we are witnessing, as well as a geographical progression. People travel along the length of the room as if they are retracing their steps through the things that have happened to them in the entire course of their lives. It is part of a 'liturgy workshop' involving people from several parish church congregations who are keen to find out how life and liturgy interact, and how each gives its life to the other. Up to now life has taken the initiative, as the people involved have offered one another understanding, support and love by talking and listening to each other. They have done this in a special way, helped by the structure of their journey which performs at least three functions.

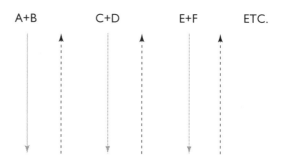

Figure 3.1 Life journeys

1   It reminds them of their life as a 'journey through time' in which particular events and situations form recognisable episodes, allowing them to perceive relationships between episodes and to make story-sense of things that have happened to them.

2   It gives them an opportunity to talk about themselves with the frankness we can permit ourselves when we speak to people whom we don't know and who don't know us, in the understanding that they are going to give us, or have already given us, the same privilege.

3   It makes this kind of sharing easier by structuring the encounter so that those taking part may attend to the way ahead, in both senses of the words, and not have to look directly at each other. (If you have ever had a longish journey either with or as a hitch-hiker, you will see the point of this.)

The process as described so far uses ritual structure to promote spontaneity. The next part is more obviously liturgical, and depends less on words to communicate its meaning. During this part there is no dialogue. At the side of the room there is a trestle table on which rows of candles have been arranged – small, free-standing candles, the kind used for night lights. People stay with their partner and prepare to make the same journey that they made to begin with. This time the one who was the listener to begin with guides his or her partner silently through the same story. As they go, she or he places a candle on the floor at certain points in the story. In this way significant places are marked by candles on the floor. These are the points that the listener perceives to be the most important stages in the speaker's journey. Then the process is reversed; the original listener is led back to the beginning by the original speaker who selects points at which to position candles.

Described like this it seems ponderous and complicated. In fact, of course, ritual and drama share the property of being better done than spoken about! The most striking thing about this process is in fact its transparency. The meaning is immediately clear, and even naturalistic movements have a significance that evades description. The actions of ritual speak louder than words because they have an immediacy which words can only signify. These movements, gestures, looks *are* what they describe. They are the action of reliving. The spoken dialogues in the first stage of this process of liturgical formation are given a kind of gestural force by their use as liturgy: the acting out of meaning in a symbolic journey allows these words and half-formed sentences, these whispered confidences and passionate avowals to stand for themselves, rescued from the contingency and provisional nature of things said in ordinary conversation. These are statements made in a context of final shape and meaning – their linguistic raggedness does not diminish their importance.

In the final stage of the process, the journey is undertaken for a third time. This is a silent pilgrimage over places that have been lived and are now being shared. Summing up the first two journeys, it is closer to liturgical action than either of them as it is a seal of mutual acceptance, a corporate offering. It is shared in a special sense, because one person's story has been accepted and validated by somebody else, not automatically or uncritically, but in a way that is empathetic and intuitive, a mutual action of taking responsibility for another person and for oneself.

Once this last part of the journey has been travelled the pairs form into a circle, holding hands. They move inwards to the centre of the circle until they are standing close together with their arms around each other's shoulders. Slowly they sway, first to the right, then left, then right, left, right, etc. They keep this up for a moment or two until it feels right to break the circle. Some of the couples go and sit somewhere by themselves until it is time to do something else.

Spiritual versus religious

There is a difference!

In the last chapter we were examining ideas about 'sacred' space – times and places which may be called holy because they are set apart to encourage personal relationship and promote a sense of wholeness which we recognise as spiritual. In itself, sacredness is usually considered to be an explicitly religious category; people who talk about it approvingly are those who hold certain religious beliefs themselves or at least respect the integrity of those who do. The last of the workshops described at the end of this chapter involved a group of church members, and although they would not (and did not) regard all of the things they did at it as being religious, they were always conscious that this was a 'Lent course'; in other words, that it had a definite religious purpose and always *implied* religion even when it was not occupied in actually saying so.

The religiousness which we are concerned with in this book is not that associated with, and taught by, theology, however. It may be the predisposition for divine revelation but it is not that revelation itself. What we are describing here is a way of answering a very obvious and well-documented need for the spiritual, which, as we have seen, is a very different thing from the state of mind which can only be satisfied by belonging to any one section of society categorisable by subscribing to a commonly held system of religious beliefs. The spirituality we are talking about here may easily be blocked, or actually destroyed, by too rigid a way of thinking and feeling about itself and the things which may 'officially' (that is by religious authorities) be held to be its business. The element of personal searching, which is a kind of spiritual hunger for a wholeness that is always just beyond one's grasp, is not exactly encouraged by those who are convinced they already know the answers to life's questions, whether their answers are religious or secular.

And yet it is a spiritual search, a hunger for spirituality. In a sense it is spirituality itself, what the word actually means. *The Concise Theological Dictionary* (Rähner and Vorgrimler, 1965) defines it as 'that which is characterised by an openness towards being and at the same time by an awareness of what itself is and is not. The two fundamental aspects of the spiritual correspond to these two opennesses – to universal being and to itself.' This is a long way from being told exactly what to believe and how to believe it, which is the specific aim of most Lent courses.

The course of workshops described attempted to break through the barrier between religion and spirituality by dealing with a religious theme in a way that encouraged the people taking part to draw on their own spiritual awareness rather than their, and their leader's, 'bible knowledge'. By spiritual awareness, I mean their experience of their own searching for wholeness, the circumstances affecting and the personal relationships which fed it and kept it alive. For us, 'the spiritual' meant many things. It was the dimension of meaning, purpose and fulfilment; the origin of an ultimate and fundamental hoping; a power beyond self which called for a response which established selfhood; a trust in others. This group of workshops represented an attempt to bypass the conflict between a religiousness which is text bound and distrusts imagination and the spirit of adventure into the unknown, and a spirituality which is too timid to allow itself to be seen except when it can claim strict religious orthodoxy. In Brian Thorne's phrase, it represents 'therapy as a spiritual vocation' (1997: 207).

In fact, this distinction between religion and spirituality is currently being threatened from two quite separate directions, sociology and depth psychology. Both of these involve an attack on what might be called the special nature of religiousness, religion regarded as a separable category, qualitatively distinct from other kinds of human experience and behaviour. The phrase 'implicit religion' was introduced by Edward Bailey (1997, 1998) to mean religion which is not spoken about, or even actually thought about, in specifically religious terms. It denotes an understanding or experience of a religious kind which is not described in language usually associated with religion. Bailey himself describes it in three ways: as 'commitment', as 'integrating foci' and as 'intensive concerns with extensive effects' (Bailey 1998). There is a widespread tendency of people and things to be or to behave in religious ways without belonging to any category of religious things or people. For instance, sociologists may talk of 'the implicit religion of football' or 'implicitly religious vegetarianism'; how religious must something be, they ask, before qualifying as a religion?

The concept of implicit religion may be seen as an attempt to come to grips with one of the most baffling and intransigent problems facing sociologists of religion – secularisation. This is the name given to the social process which, it is claimed, has somehow superseded religion as a significant factor in western awareness and in the social life that affects and is affected by that awareness. There is no disagreement about the fact that religious institutions no longer play the part that they did in social life; and many people in the west assume that this is the inevitable result of widespread education in scientific ways of explaining the world and scientistic propaganda about superior epistemologies to traditional religious ones. 'Official' religion itself has largely become the preoccupation of enthusiasts, people who do not expect to be understood by the wider society and take refuge in scriptural warnings that to be authentically religious is always to be a minority. Nevertheless, genuine religious behaviour still exists on a widespread scale as a social force. The only difference is that the objects of its devotion have changed and it calls itself by different names. Worship itself, both as a state of mind and a social activity, is far from being dead. It is simply that the socio-formative functions of religion are being carried out by other social institutions.

Implicit religion is not to be thought of as an ersatz form of 'the real thing'. It constitutes an alternative way of dealing with the same personal and social state of affairs that gives rise to explicitly religious expression and belonging. For Bailey, implicitness does not imply an abandoning of the central realities which are the heart of religious behaviour, but a determination to express religious commitment in a social and cultural climate that is constantly aversive to it. From this point of view implicitness signifies a greater depth and toughness than explicitness does, simply because it demonstrates the survival of attitudes and behaviour characteristic of religious belonging within a culture that refuses to consider them significant. 'Implicit' is not a disguise but a validation. What is being validated is a dimension of humanness that is vitally important for any kind of sociological account, particularly the kind that dismisses the importance of religion as a structural factor in contemporary social consciousness.

Psychologically speaking there is no clear division between spirituality and religion. The difference, as Durkheim (1915) recognised when he turned his attention to Australian aboriginal societies, is one of organisation of thought. Spirituality is essentially a shared experience. Even hermits pray for and acknowledge the prayers of others, and C.G. Jung was convinced that our own 'private' spirituality is simply a personal manifestation of a shared dimension of psychological co-inherence existing at the unconscious level among all human beings and uniting them by means of the collective unconscious (1968). Even the organisational difference between structure and informality is extremely blurred, as 'spontaneous' spiritual awareness becomes institutionalised and religious belonging erupts unexpectedly in outbursts of spiritual activity that surprise everyone, particularly those involved.

Psychologists as a whole have tended to think of spiritual (and consequently religious) experience as abnormal, something slightly apart from ordinary psychological functioning. Freud, for instance, regarded it as an artefact, created by the ego in order to make the pressure exerted by the superego more bearable; on its own, however, as a definable psychic reality, it does not and cannot exist, there being no room for it within the tightly organised economy of the individual psyche, according to which everything that happens of a psychological nature remains strictly 'within the system' and gains its psychological reality from this fact.

The evidence produced by Jung as to the existence of a psychological dimension, operating at the most fundamental level, which is actually shared – the 'collective unconscious' – has led psychologists of the transpersonal school to think again about the possibility of regarding spirituality as a psychological function in its own right, rather than as the by-product or epiphenomenon of something else which is scientifically more 'real'. Certainly spirituality is un-analysable; but, says Ken Wilber, this is because human psychic structure has not yet evolved to a point at which it is capable of comprehending its workings. Even now, however, psychologists must learn to take account of 'experiences involving an expansion or extension of consciousness beyond the usual ego boundaries and beyond the limitation of time and space' (Grof 1979: 155). Such experiences will in time become intelligible to men and women to the same extent that 'normal' psychic experience is at our present level of evolution. Transpersonal psychology points to a time when we will have evolved as far as truth itself, and when psychology and religion will be recognisable as one and the same. This, of course, cannot be assessed in the way that our current psychological life may be understood, but like psychoanalysis itself, it may be theorised about in advance, the only difference being that Wilber's transpersonal map of psychic development is considerably more ambitious than Freud's intrapsychic one, involving as it does the eventual divinisation of the entire human race (Wilber 1981).

Psychology, then, need not be private in the sense of individualistic; it need not reduce either personal spirituality or organised religion to a disguised form of something entirely intra- rather than interpsychic. As we have already seen, the psychology of groups must take account of the phenomenon of shared spirituality. On the other hand, religion may be implicit rather than explicit, and within a secular society often is so. Whether implicit or explicit, however, it originates in spiritual aware-ness that is shared among groups of people: group spirituality must take account of group psychology. The ritual experiences of groups need not be considered to be explicitly religious, and this is not how they are usually interpreted by the people taking part in them.

- It was a ritual, if you like, but not really a religious one. It was something we shared as a group.
- It just seemed a good way of showing how important some things are in your life without trying to find words for it.
- I suppose using candles made it all a bit like church, but that's why they were used, isn't it, to help us see how important it was, what we were doing I mean.
- Do you mean the candles? I don't care, I love candles anyway. They show you care about something.
- If you mean the kind of ritual which is just for show, it definitely wasn't that.

Implicit or explicit?

> There is a connection between spiritual awareness and the kind of experience described as implicitly religious!

Ideas about 'who we are' and 'who other people are' belong closely together in the way that we look at life. The question about 'who God is' is intrinsic to both. As has been so often said, it is the matter that concerns us most in life – whether or not we may actually believe we know who he is. People who believe in God go so far as to define him in these terms, as 'the most important thing in my life'. Those who do not have this knowledge (or aren't sure whether they have it or not) are often conscious of having what has been called a 'God-shaped gap' which plays more or less the same part in their thinking. In other words, it acts as the final authority so far as the value and importance of everything else is concerned. What they think about the things that happen to them, the people they meet, the purpose and importance of life itself is governed by this central authority which, for them, takes the form of a question – or rather *the* question.

For still more people the central authority is only implicitly religious: they do not affirm either God or what he would stand for if he existed. Nevertheless, if they are examined closely, as in the studies in implicit religion carried out by Edward Bailey, these people are willing to admit that there is something or someone who plays this organising role in their personal view of life; an all-important factor in their awareness that is able to draw from the kind of 'ultimate concern' that is Paul Tillich's definition of faith (1962b: 1 ff.). This central commitment may take a whole range of forms in particular people – extreme devotion to a football team, total identification with a political philosophy, an ideal of professional conduct, responsibility to one's own family as the source of all real value and significance. However (or more precisely *wherever*) it is recognised, it provides their life with the central focus it needs in order to make unified sense of all the many things that happen in it.

The psychologist George Kelly called these foci of personal meaning 'core constructs'. They are the pegs on which our appreciation of life hangs. Because of the intensity of the significance which belongs to them, our most critical concerns affect all the interconnected parts of our life, growing less powerful and less effective the more peripheral they are. These are the cords that bind our individual worlds together. They may not seem to exert much influence over the ordinary everyday things we feel, do and plan; nevertheless they remain the psychological driving force that gives purpose to life, its actions, experiences and intentions, allowing us to know who we are. Because we know where particular factors in our world belong in our 'personal construct system', we know where we ourselves belong, and are able therefore to 'position' other people in the world as we see it. Kelly points out that because we have first-hand knowledge of giving shape to our own worlds by ranking our experiences in order of their relevance to what, for us, is *really* important, we can imagine the same sort of thing going on for other people as well, and take this into account in the way we act and react towards them. This kind of 'sociality' is demonstrated most clearly in the inter-relatedness which binds together the individual members of a group.

Telling my story

The opportunity of 'make spiritual sense' of things that have happened to you has a psychologically healing effect.

It is immediately obvious how crucial imagination is in the process Kelly describes. It is imagination that allows us to share our worlds and create a construct system which is genuinely shared. In Kelly's own words 'To the extent that one person construes the construction processes of another, he may play a role in a social process involving the other person' (1963: 95). And so we return to the construction of stories, this time at the most basic level of all.

The stories that people tell about themselves contain a good deal of information that would be of interest to anybody who wanted to find out how they saw themselves and their world. Although, when we are telling our life story to someone else we try to be as objective as possible, the narrative which emerges is always influenced by our views about the relative importance of the people and events we describe and their significance to the story as a whole. From this point of view our realism is, to say the least, selective. We use our dramatic sense to choose what to put in and leave out, even sometimes to rearrange the order in which things actually happened. In fact, our sense of personal drama acknowledges a higher order than that required by historical accuracy, namely the demand of a kind of meaning we ourselves recognise as inclusive. The ruling principle of the life story turns out to be a certain kind of relationship among the things that happen to us, one that can only be described as 'personal significance'.

Life stories are put together in order to draw attention to that relationship. Our personal sense of the significance of these things is the reason why they are included in the story we tell about ourselves. And this is a reflexive process, one which goes on increasing the meaning of the tale we are telling simply by the action of telling it. This is what the anthropologist Edmund Leach refers to as 'metonymy' (1976). It happens when we become aware of the symbolic content of things we are talking (or even thinking) about; their reference to a meaning which we perceive to be over-arching and inclusive. Thinking and talking about these matters tends to make them more tangible to us. The process is a reflexive one because the authority of what the symbol refers to feeds back to the events perceived as symbolic, making them more real and authentic – more historically valid in fact.

The essential thing to recognise is that these symbols are not ideas that have been devised in accordance with a ready made 'plan of reality', but *events*, things that have happened to people in their own lives and those of the people who are important to them. Ideas, cultural codes designed for the interpretation of life, are obviously important to us, governing the ways in which our experience is expressed and communicated, but the subject matter, the thing remembered and relived is the substance of our past life as we perceive it here and now in the part it is playing within our experience of the present. This is the human thing that provides a stepping stone into the unknown: the unknown past, influencing as it does both present and future. What we know and can remember, and the *form* in which we are able to remember it, carries us nearer to realities we are not yet ready to envisage. It is a powerful token of those realities.

Those whose job involves listening to other people give an account of their lives – psychotherapists, clergy, policemen and doctors for example – are often conscious of the way the stories that they hear from clients, parishioners, suspects and patients change the more they are repeated. This is not so surprising in the case of people suspected of a crime; but what is noticeable is the degree to which it happens with those who are not really conscious that they are doing it. Sometimes stories become more confused as the narrator's grasp on their own sense of identity has grown looser over time. Sometimes they improve greatly, and their improvement as stories reflects a personality that is rediscovering its integrity. When someone says 'It has helped me to talk about this. Thank you for listening!', the listener knows that an important process has been taking place within the speaker's construct system towards greater flexibility of thought processes, a more highly integrated and more organised view of the world. There has been a change towards a greater awareness of, and a more positive relationship with, something or someone whose presence at the centre of this person's life has given it new meaning, making it a proper life with a proper life story.

The shape of a story

The significance of a story is inherent in its shape. This is an archetype of meaning which gives weight to our attempts to order our perception of the world we live in.

It is important to recognise that the *shape* of a story reflects the urgency of the meaning it communicates. It also contributes to the clarity with which meanings are held, affecting their ability to direct our lives, and giving our stories even more significance, so that as time goes on they need less and less editing. Psychotherapists report that patients whose narratives are jumbled and incoherent are able to tell their life story much more succinctly and powerfully when their state of mind has improved. Some of them point to the therapeutic effect of encouraging unhappy and anxious people to spend their time thinking about what has been creative and valuable in their lives and to try to tell their stories from that point of view.

This is easier said than done, of course: in a sense this suggestion represents the problem rather than the solution. It is precisely because we find ourselves unable to lay hold of life in this way that we feel anxious and unhappy. Because we have lost hold of the reality of what we have done and suffered we seem to have lost our sense of who we really are, we can no longer say with any certainty, I am the one who achieved, discovered, completed, went through, whatever it was we did in the past. We have no sense of having managed to get where we are. Something prevents us from making the past *our* past.

There are, of course, things we have done, and that have been done to us, that we try to forget. This would appear to be true of everybody. Because it is too painful to remember these things and the feelings they give rise to, we acknowledge their presence reluctantly, taking care not to think about them very much, or ever if we can help it. Other things, however, get wiped out altogether, and any systematic attempt we make to remember them simply has the effect of strengthening our resistance against them. In Freudian language they represent material that has been efficiently repressed, completely removed from our conscious awareness. However they are regarded, they constitute areas of life on which we have managed to turn our backs.

This is, however, material of the very greatest importance for constructing our 'house of life'. It consists of words, discoveries, experiences, judgements, relating to the very source of life's meaning and purpose. It cannot be blotted out without affecting things that draw meaning and significance from their association with it. These 'lower level constructs' may be allowed to remain within the system, as they had no immediate reference to whatever has been taken out – indeed their association may be at second, third or fourth hand. Nevertheless, they constitute knowledge, understanding, a particular way of perceiving reality which belongs to our personal construct system; which in a sense *is* the system, because, understood from this point of view, the way in which we make sense of what happens to us is itself an interchange between meaning and experience, the first moving downwards to the business of living, the second upwards to the source of value.

No wonder, then, that emotionally destructive experiences and events have a draining effect on our sense of the world's reality, seeing that the ways in which we ourselves manage to make it real have been cut off at source; when for us, love, joy, belonging, fulfilment, the peace of mind that comes with security, have been ruled out of court because of their association with events that life has made unthinkable. According to Marcuse (1984), Freud drew attention to the disorganised, incoherent stories told him by his patients before he began treating them. These stories had somehow to be given the kind of coherence that could only come when those patients were willing and able to take responsibility for them. 'At the end – at the successful end – one has come into possession of one's own story' (quoted by Cox and Theilgaard 1987: 60). This can involve an immense amount of work as 'Psychotherapy is concerned with a story which is so disturbing that however painful the telling may be, it must be attempted' (Cox and Theilgaard 1987: 59). Until we have managed to restore contact with what has been quite systematically forgotten, our original sense of things belonging together, of having something of the greatest importance to refer to and be connected with, will remain beyond our grasp.

Sometimes this is a relatively short-lived experience. In some cases things seem to come back of their own accord, as if the organism had taken steps to defend itself against the impact of intolerable events by simply suspending its awareness until it can tolerate something of the actuality of whatever has happened without too great an emotional reaction, too much pain, in fact. Sometimes it takes a more sustained effort, although not necessarily one that involves a head-on approach. Again, this is something that professional listeners learn to recognise.

> I can remember one young woman who came to see me in hospital because she wanted someone to listen to her story. Her marriage had broken down and her two small children taken into care: 'I just want you to listen because so many things have been happening. I can't make sense of my life, and I want you to help me.' I couldn't help her. I couldn't make any sense of it either. She was only young, in her late thirties, but more things seemed to have happened to her than most people experience in an entire life-time. Some of what had happened to her, an isolated incident which had occurred

some weeks after disaster had struck, had stuck in her mind and she kept repeating it as if it somehow held the key to everything else. I could see that there was a connection between this and the main incidents in her story; but I couldn't really see how it could be anything like so important, so vital for her story, as she obviously thought it was. I said I was puzzled about this; why did she lay such stress on it? It couldn't have caused the marital breakdown, could it? I was sorry, but I didn't really understand what she was getting at. I'd like to help, of course, but . . .

The look she gave me held both frustration and contempt. At least, that is how I received it; it may have only been pity for my obtuseness. She got up and left the room without saying a word. I didn't expect to see her again. Perhaps it really had been pity, however, because eventually she did come back to see me; but not yet.

At last, six months after the original interview, she felt she was ready to answer my question. She sat down, had a cup of coffee, and proceeded to put me in the picture. This time things were much clearer, much more identifiable as a story. The incident which had stood out so clearly because it was so extremely significant to her, while seeming unconnected with the other events she had described, had fallen into place with quite remarkable effect as the keystone of the narrative, the factor that enabled it to function properly as a story. For weeks after the events she had described, she had been carrying all the parts of her puzzle around with her and not known how to begin the task of putting them all together'. One thing she did know, however. In trying to 'take it all in', she ran the risk of coming up against a good deal of psychological conflict. The connections were difficult because they were connections with pain. The incident stood out because its meaning was too painful to be clearly presented, and had to take on some kind of disguise. The incoherence and confusion were not only caused by pain, that of the breakdown in her family relationships, they were also a way of protecting herself from pain – the agony she was bound to feel once she clearly understood all that had actually happened.

(Hospital chaplain, personal communication)

Why had this woman struggled so hard to get her meaning – or lack of meaning – across to the chaplain? Why, considering the pain involved in remembering, was she so relieved when things became clearer and she could remember again? The answer, of course, lies in the fact that the need to understand is so fundamental to human experience that it takes priority over almost every other human need, even that of avoiding discomfort. Avoidance of pain is of course an immediate response, and if meaning is too painful, measures will be taken to change it and make it less so. Sooner or later, however, it will find expression and fulfilment.

Within the sphere of human meaning, these two things belong together, so that to express a need to understand already implies a conscious effort towards understanding, and at a lower level of awareness a process of cognitive construction which will eventually come up with an answer to the problem, a resolution of the 'cognitive dissonance' caused by the disturbing pressure exerted by the presence of unanswered questions. The brain is a problem-solving mechanism; and one of the ways it solves problems concerning the meaning of life involves the creation *and reformulation* of stories.

This is not to say that these stories are simply fantasy and have no basis in actual events in their historical order. Nevertheless we are the ones who put them together, we are masters of our stories, not they of us. This is reasonable enough. The underlying meaning of life is not entirely dependent upon the order in which things happen to us – as Kierkegaard says 'Life is lived in the future and understood in the past' (1959). In a sense, events are the raw material out of which we create our own meaning – with a little guidance from the stories of others, whatever form these may take – as theories, doctrines, political manifestos, etc. The Christian gospels are examples of stories which have this guiding and shaping effect upon our own self-accounting.

> The young woman came back to me to celebrate the fact that instead of a jumble of memories and feelings, she now had a story she could tell herself. The incident she had told me about in such a frantic way to begin with turned out to be the heart of the matter, as she had sensed all along. With the passage of time, she had felt able to look closely at its meaning and implications, instead of simply turning the event itself over and over in her mind. When she could bear to probe further, the solution came quite easily. With it came the possibility of meaning for the whole series of events which had stunned and bewildered her. It was the presence of something that didn't 'fit' and had to be worked on that enabled her to identify her pain and eventually come to terms with it.

In this case the process of reorganisation of meaning seems to have simply involved the passage of time. Perhaps it could have been assisted in some way; perhaps it was. In some cases, certainly, it needs special encouragement. This woman had gone a lot of the way by herself, working hard to arrive at a past she could make sense of and learn to live with. Stephen Crites calls this 'approaching a past'. He says it is the way in which an individual becomes a *self*. Selfhood is not something given from the beginning. It is something we achieve by interpreting our experience and building on our interpretations. Thus, 'Self is a kind of aesthetic construct, recollected in and with the life of experience in narrative fashion . . . and the more complete the story, the more integrated the self.' He goes on to comment that 'The poignant search for roots that is such a prominent feature of our rootless age testifies to the acute unease a human being can feel without a coherent story of a personal past.' He contrasts contemporary western society with times and places where 'a person's life-story is so powerfully supported by the ethos and mythos of the community' that people think of themselves 'as if they were as highly defined and constant in time as the house they have always lived in' (1986: 162).

This is not in any way to suggest that experience of actual events is not important for the self's understanding of itself. However it is how the self uses this essential raw material that determines the kind of story we tell ourselves about ourselves. We can use our story-telling skill to convince ourselves of the truth of things we are really aware of being untrue. In a sense we have to do this in order to clear the story space we need of all the material that is irrelevant 'All storytelling tries to deny and be silent about just as much as it strains to convey' (Wyatt cited by Sarbin 1986: 208). As in all art, the realism of the personal story is selective; but, as in all art, its truth is emotional or aesthetic rather than literal, and self stories which are to be convincing must somehow reflect emotional truthfulness if they are to possess the sincerity they need to convince their listeners and, of course, the speakers themselves.

Narrative and world construction

From a therapeutic point of view the most important characteristic of the personal story is in fact its nature as a construct. At one level, the basic one, it is always ritualised – in other words presented in a form in which the underlying message may be presented as graphically as possible, because it represents a personal view of the meaning and significance of human experience. If the meaning and significance can be modified in any way, the experience will change retrospectively; and this entire equation depends upon a view that is personal and can consequently be changed. Personal stories are modifiable rituals. Certainly facts which cannot be changed lie at the root of many, if not most, of our anxieties about life; we are aware that things exist which govern our experience in ways we have no control over at all. And so we tell ourselves that we live in 'the real world' and must suffer the consequences of the fact.

This is true, of course, but this real world is one in which our happiness is not, in the final analysis, a matter of fact (or 'the facts') but of interpretation. The state of mind in which we approach life depends upon how we construe the truth about what has happened to us. If the realism of these events is too great for us to bear, we need to convince ourselves of the specious nature of their ability to control the way we look at life. Somehow or other they must not be allowed to impose on us a single inflexible interpretation of their meaning and significance. The way we do this is by subjecting the facts, whatever they may be, to the authority even greater than theirs, some kind of transcendent truthfulness that can only be portrayed symbolically.

The fact that we can so often bring this off is actually a sign of strength, not weakness. Human beings are creatures who are able to change the world for themselves by altering their attitude towards it. 'To the living creature', says George Kelly, 'the universe is real, but it is not inexorable, unless he chooses to construe it that way' (1963: 8). As Epictetus, the stoic philosopher put it, 'Men are not disturbed by things but by the view they take of them' (1983, para. 5). Quite early in our life experience, we discover that we can change the way things are for us by locating them in a revised version of our life narrative by expanding the narrative to accommodate them. This does not mean that we have to deny their importance in any way – quite the opposite, because we have to take proper account of them in order to move on from them into a new stage in the story. Events that are so traumatic that our current arrangements for living, and dying, are completely shattered by them, and we are stopped short in our tracks, can come to signify in retrospect not the end of our story but simply the culmination of a stage in its plot. Without this the story cannot continue and develop. What once appeared to make nonsense of the whole enterprise of story telling turns out to be the necessary condition for a new and better story, in which genuine endings allowed beginnings which were really new, not merely an extension of the former state of affairs, and old questions received new answers. We develop a sense of what Havens has called our 'history-laden present' (cited by Cox and Theilgaard 1987).

This, of course, is the shape of the stories we tell as well as those we live. It is the shape of folk tales, myths and fairy stories, as well as novels, short stories and epic poems. As we have seen, it is the basic order of events contained in religious rituals of all kinds. Experiences of disintegration are contained by the imagery of wholeness; questions about the meaning of life and the unintelligibility of human experience are answered in the light of a greater understanding, a wider view.

As we have seen, in dramatherapy this kind of healing by story provides opportunities for the healing of stories. In these workshops vivid experiences of encounter with meaning are the building blocks for new stories and the reconstruction of old ones. They were devised as a way of deconstructing self-narratives which had become rigidly attached to particular interpretations of what had happened to the narrators. The past can hang as heavily round our necks as the Ancient Mariner's albatross.

Spirituality rituals

At the beginning of this chapter we were looking at a group exercise to explore the experience of exchanging personal narratives. This took the form of a 'spirituality ritual'. It was a ceremony performed in order to represent a spiritual reality – that of the meaning of human lives expressed in personal stories. Because life is a historical process this ceremony embodied a linear movement through space. It was described at this point in the book because the chapter as a whole is about the way we are conscious of our lives as moving through time. This rite uses the language of space to present the language of time.

Ritual itself, however, is not time-bound; the significance of using movement and gesture to express shared meaning transcends limitations of time and space. Spirituality rituals do not concern themselves solely with historical time or geographical space.

Here are some 'meaningful ceremonies' which use different kinds of ordinary human experience to embody a sense of extraordinary significances:

Depth (moving inwards to the centre)

1   Stand in as wide a circle as possible, leaving as much space as you can between yourself and whoever is standing to your left and right. Hold a baton in your hand.

2   Turn left or right to face one of the people next to you. (This means that successive people have to turn alternative ways, so that you

end up with a circle consisting of pairs of people who are now face to face, while remaining some distance from each other.)

3   Take it in turns to speak to your partner, saying who you are and why you have come to the workshop. When you have both done this exchange your batons.

4   Take two paces sideways towards the centre of the circle, thus making it smaller. Now tell your partner something else about yourself – the kind of person you think you are, the kind of people you like being with. When you have done this, let your partner tell you about him or herself in the same way. Exchange batons again.

5   Take two more paces sideways. Tell your partner something about yourself which you feel is more personal. Then listen to your partner and exchange batons.

6   Take the necessary number of sideways steps until everyone in the group is within touching distance of everyone else.

7   Turn to the person behind you and look at each other. You needn't speak but give them your baton.

8   Stand as closely to everyone as you can, with your arms round one another. Sway to the music.

9   At a signal (a gong?) move backwards into the positions occupied at the beginning, when you were standing 'alone' in the wider circle.

10 A candle is placed in the centre. Spend a few minutes looking at it and thinking about the rite you have been involved in. What name would you give it? Share your ideas with the group.

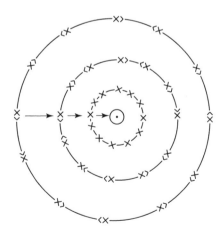

Figure 3.2 Depths

Ascents (the cliff face)

1   Stand in a line along one wall of the room, facing into the room. If you are at one of the two ends of the row, take a candle and hold it.

2   When you hear the signal, move forward a pace (or two according to the size of the room), leaving the two who are holding candles standing in the same place.

3   If you are now at one or other end of the row, take a candle and light it from the person behind you who blows his or her candle out.

4   When you hear the signal again, move forward once more, leaving the two people with candles behind you.

5   If you are now at one or other end of the row, take a candle and light it from the person behind you who will now blow their candle out.

6   Continue in this way until there are only three people in the row. If you are the one in the middle wait for the signal and move to the apex of the triangle, lighting your candle from one of the two people below you, both of whom now blow their candles out.

7   Stand silently for a few moments listening to the music, everybody facing up to the apex, where the one with the lighted candle stands facing outward as the spearhead of the group.

8   Starting from the two people next to the candle bearer, light your candle from the person next in line above you.

9   When all the candles are lit, place yours on the spot where you are standing and go and sit in a circle round the flaming pyramid you have made.

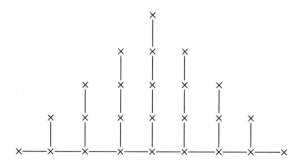

Figure 3.3 Ascents

Vulnerability (Scylla and Charybdis)

1 Divide into two tightly knit groups in which people have their arms round one another's shoulders or waists.
2 As a group, take possession of your half of the room by moving round it to stake your claim to it.
3 As a group, come to the edge of your territory opposite the other group and stand there swaying, almost but not quite touching their group.
4 One person at a time, leave your group and join up with your opposite number from the other group.
5 As a pair, make your way between the two groups.
6 When you have managed to 'thread the needle', join the other couples who have made the journey and form a ring round the space where the rival groups were opposed to each other.
7 Hold hands in the ring. Sway gently one way and then the other. Do this gently so that you can find the point of balance for the group.

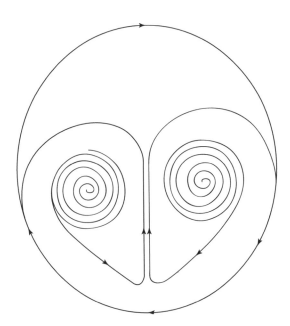

Figure 3.4 Vulnerability

Struggle (the tree and the stream, the rock and the sea)

1   Divide into two groups, one holding hands and standing in a line, the other standing together in a tight circle, each person holding on to the two adjacent people.

2   If you are a member of the first group, follow your leader as she/he leads you round the room, gradually moving closer to the second group who are standing together in the middle of the room without moving.

3   If you are a member of the second group, try to stand your ground as the first group pushes against you. Tighten your hold on one another. Now try to stretch your arms out to include as many people as you can reach and hug them to yourself as the first group surrounds your group and tries to uproot you. They will struggle with you. Hold your ground and when you are all ready, hold out your hands to them and welcome them into your group.

4   Absorb the ring of people around you.

5   Take somebody's hand and lead them out away from the knot of people. As they come out they will lead someone else out, and so on, until there is a string of people, all holding hands.

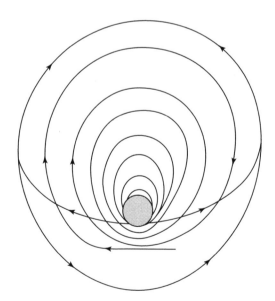

Figure 3.5 Struggle

6   Follow the line of people round the room as it forms into a circle. You are all still holding hands.

7   Squeeze the hand of the person on your left; wait until the squeeze returns to you from the right. Repeat this, going in the other direction.

Eternity ('I saw Eternity the other night . . . ')

1   Form two concentric rings of people, the inner containing fewer people than the outer and holding lighted candles in their hands.

2   Members of the inner group turn outwards to face the outer circle. Begin to move in a clockwise direction.

3   Members of the outer group hold hands and move round in the other direction, facing inwards.

4   Move round in concentric circles, in opposite directions but at the same speed.

5   Vary the speeds at which the two circles are revolving. (This is done by the outer circle going faster or slower while the inner one continues to move at the speed it began with.)

6   Members of the inner group – as the outer group moves round you, start to give them your candles. Go on doing this until you have given them all away.

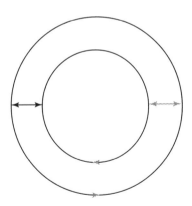

          ········ GIVE CANDLES TO OUTER CIRCLE

          ———   GIVE HANDS TO INNER CIRCLE,
                    DRAW INTO OUTER CIRCLE

Figure 3.6 Eternity

7   Members of the outer group – take the hand of the person who has given you their candle and draw them into the outer circle, to dance round it with you.

These are a few examples of the kind of ritual movement that are the staple of the 'spirituality workshops' described in the next section. They are not workshops, simply expressive ceremonies which form part of a larger and less formal occasion, one which is more exploratory and spontaneous, and less focused. These rites are, in fact, a vivid way of encapsulating something diffuse and evasive which somehow escapes literal description. They are, in fact, acted symbols. They take the form of stories without words; only the one described at the beginning of this chapter actually involves any kind of spoken autobiographical material. The focusing effect of ritual provides a way of clearing a space for the meaning which inspires both personal stories and the self-awareness of the group as a whole – in other words, its own story. Things are encompassed here which cannot adequately be described. Life is rescued from contingency and incompleteness and becomes a formal expression of the principle of meaning, which is actually the underlying form of things, the fundamental presence of *shape* in both ideas and words. Here, the formal is used to express form. It does so by embodying it – which is precisely how it occurs in life.

These ceremonies, and every imaginable rite of such a kind, are ways of presenting prototypical themes by embodying them in meaningful action and movement. In effect rituals like these interrupt the flow of time in order to introduce at least the idea, and sometimes the experience, of eternity. In this way, the progression, which is our life story as this is spread over so many months, years and decades, becomes a single unitary experience – an event in depth. This imaged 'meaning of life' is shared because it corresponds to the life experience of women and men throughout the world.

One way of expressing this fundamental recognition of the kind of truth which belongs to simply being human is to say that it is *archetypal*. Archetypes are picture stories dealing with experiences, awarenesses, kinds of understanding which are essentially shared by the entire human race. In archetypes this understanding is revealed as corporate. The aim of ritual is to take this unconscious knowledge and incorporate it within the conscious awareness of individuals and groups, and individuals *through* groups.

Spirituality workshops

Three workshops about animals, birds, fish and insects.

I What shall we do with people?

1 Circle the space, saying hello to people as you move round.
2 Still moving round, take on the role of an insect, bird, fish or animal.
3 Find your special 'habitat', then join up with the others in the centre of the room.
4 Form a circle and play the following game. Take turns to say what kind of creature you are and show the gesture by which you can be recognised. Now go round the ring, beginning with the first creature and ending with the last one, taking turns to show your 'call sign' (identifying gesture). The game itself begins when somebody makes someone else's call sign. If you see your sign being made you first of all answer by making it yourself, and then make someone else's; they have to reply with theirs before making someone else's – and so it goes on for as long as you like.
5 The leader reads a story about a bird, fish, animal or insect.
6 Join up with three or four others and take some time creating a short drama (two to three minutes) which includes three main characters: the Lawgiver (male), the Wise Creature (female), the Trickster (a player of games), and which is about a problem concerning the relationship between people and creatures of other kinds.
7 Appoint a spokescreature to share the drama with the others or, better still, act it for them. When you have done this, place a token from your drama in the centre of the room.
8 Compose a group rhythm and stand round the pile of tokens, beating your rhythm out in unison.
9 Write a joint letter to the human race, summoning it to appear before the Court of Creatures on such and such a date. Give one of the creatures represented the job of delivering this. He or she will be the Messenger.
10 Use your call signs to signal farewell to everyone.

II The trial

1 Say hello to people 'as yourself'.
2 Move round the room as the creature you are impersonating and greet the other creatures as you meet them.

3   Pay attention as the Messenger calls you to order. The Messenger gives each of the four kinds of creature – animals, birds, fish and insects – its own 'group call'.

4   Start making your own call and gather up together with your own group, so that there are four groups of creatures, each occupying a different part of the room.

5   Work with the other members of your group to develop a characteristic dance, using the various percussion and wind instruments available. When you are ready, perform your dance for the other creatures, who will stand in a circle around you.

6   Clear the circle, the trial is about to begin. The Messenger tells everybody that the human being has refused to appear before them. She/he places four representative objects in the centre of the circle: a briefcase, a teapot, a mobile phone and a driving licence (for instance).

7   Join with everybody present, apart from the Messenger, in taking on the following personae in succession: the Lawgiver (pronouncing on right and wrong), the Wise Creature (possessing insight and knowledge of life), the Trickster (an anarchic character, with street wisdom).

8   Speak to humanity from the point of view of these three archetypes, waiting for people to finish talking as the first of them before moving on to the second and then the third. When you have finished, the Messenger will attempt to reply for humanity.

9   Decide with your group whether you are willing or able to forgive the human race. Show the degree of your acceptance by placing a candle at the appropriate distance from the representative objects in the centre of the room.

10   Sit silently and listen to the music.

11   Say goodbye, first to your group members, then to everyone.

III The parliament of creatures

1   When you have said hello to people, take on your role as a non-human creature.

2   Sit in a wide circle, as you were doing in the last workshop.

3   Take turns to say your name and the creature whose part you are playing.

4   Shout your group call. Which group shouts loudest?

5   Start to move round the room in character. Use your group call to find your fellow group members and settle with them in the part of the room you selected in the first of these workshops.

6   As a group, prepare your message for the whole assembly about what you consider is your contribution to life and the universe.

7   Write your joint message down in large letters on a piece of card. Use the materials provided – finger paints, crayons, modelling clay, coloured paper etc. – to illustrate what you have written.

8   Place your card in the centre of the room.

9   Walk round, looking at the cards and reading the messages presented on them.

10   Go back to the circle and start to dance round as the creatures you represent. Begin slowly and simply so that everyone can join in.

11   Sit down and listen to a story read by the leader.

12   Say goodbye to everybody.

The following is a more explicitly religious workshop format (i.e. a series of workshops organised around a single, explicitly religious theme).

Journey to the cross

The six workshops briefly described here represent a series of Lent meetings shared by four local churches (Anglican, Baptist, Methodist and Roman Catholic). They concentrate on exploring people's consciousness of eternity within the present moment, using the power of metaphor to 'touch the heart and awaken the emotions'. Although taking place more than two years ago, I still experience them extremely vividly, mainly because they concentrate on experience and not argument, registering at the level of feeling rather than intellect. They were happenings that involved me before I was able to draw conclusions from them.

Although I myself acted as leader, I designed the sessions to depend on the imagination and creativity of the people taking part, most of whom were, to begin with, slightly startled by this approach to setting up a Lent course. I had carefully let it be known that things would be arranged rather differently from usual; for one thing, there certainly wouldn't be rows of chairs facing a lectern. This being the case, would anyone actually come? As it turned out an average of forty people attended all six sessions.

Session one: 'wells of living water'

People sat on chairs arranged in a wide circle, taking in the whole floor space at a church community centre. The leader explained the idea behind the sessions, which were to be about personal discovery rather than instruction. This didn't mean that people were going to be expected to do or say things they were uncomfortable with. It wouldn't be embarrassing. It would be fun. He said a short extempore prayer, asking God to bless the session.

1 Stay sitting in a circle. Each person says his or her name, plus two other words – one describing what it feels like to be here, and one characterising Lent. Somebody, a volunteer, reads the story about Jesus and the Samaritan woman, from John 4.5–20 ('You haven't got a bucket').

2 Walk round the room finding as many different places to go as you can. Imagine that somewhere in this room there is water. So go and find it for yourself. What kind of water is it? A river, a well, the sea itself? What's it like there? Are there waves, rocks, strong currents? Is it a deep well, hewn out of the rock? Have a good look. What would you like to do with it, do you think? It welcomes you to make contact with it. So why not do that . . . dabble your toes or cup your hands; plunge in and swim around. What does it feel like? How does it taste? Why don't you try splashing somebody? (After all, you can't hurt them.)

3 Form into a small group with four other people. Tell the others in your group about the water you have been imagining. Did it remind you of anything in your life? If it did, you can share some of your water with them. Mime doing this by taking them to the place in the room where the water is and showing it to them. Let them lead you to the parts of the room where they, too, discovered water.

4 Move back into the large circle. There's some music playing, so listen to it quietly for a moment or two. Does it sound like water at all? (Actually it was the waterfall scherzo from the 'Manfred' Symphony by Tchaikovsky.) Have you anything you feel you would like to share with the whole group? Any memories or reflections? How did the water make you feel?

5 Mime something about water, using the space in the centre of the group to do this. (It was some time before anybody summoned up the courage to do this.) Join up with the other people's mimes, so that you create a moving picture of what water can be like.

6 Move round in a circle, each person following their partner. After you have completed the circuit of the room twice, stand still. Everybody in the circle takes one step sideways towards the centre, turns to his or her neighbour, saying goodbye to them. You can hug them if they don't mind. Otherwise be sure to shake their hand.

Session two: the living past

There was less movement in this session, which tended to be quieter and more reflective. Perhaps people were still thinking about last week's session, or the sight of the other members of the group reminded them of things they had been feeling then. The leader started things off with a short prayer.

1 Sitting in the large circle turn to the people on both sides of you and say hello to them. Then find somebody you haven't met properly and go across and greet them, telling them your name and asking them theirs.

2 Still in the large circle join in the game explained to you by the leader. It is called 'Indian Chief'.

This game involves everybody present. Each person takes it in turn to adopt the name of an imaginary chieftain which is immediately recognisable by her or his title. (In other words, you have to behave in a way that suggests the name you have chosen – e.g. 'Big Chief Throwing Spear' throws an imaginary spear at the same time as mentioning her or his name.) After everybody has decided who they are going to 'be' (which isn't really very hard to do, because you can choose to be 'Big Chief Doing Nothing' or even 'Big Chief I'm Off Home' if you want!) the game itself can begin. In this people communicate with one another across the circle by miming their own adopted name, following this by imitating someone else's. When the other person sees their own 'name' being mimed, they answer by repeating it to show they've received the message. Then they themselves imitate another person's 'call sign' – and so on. It is a game that seems simple, but causes a good deal of hilarity because no one ever gets it quite right. It was designed to be about identity, role playing and fun – mainly fun. When everybody is tired of it, the leader asks for a volunteer to read the Bible passage, which is Ecclesiastes 3.

3 Find a partner and get them to promise to keep their eyes shut (if they're not sure they can do this, use a handkerchief or a scarf to blindfold them). Take their arm and lead them around the room, in and out of other people (who are also leading or being led). When you have spent three or four minutes doing this, swap roles so that 'leaders' are now 'led', and continue for the same amount of time. Then go and sit down somewhere with your partner. What did it feel like to be led? To lead?

4   With your partner follow an imaginary path across the room. As you walk along, tell them the story of your own life journey, using the markers provided (small candles or pebbles) to indicate staging posts – crucial changes of direction – along the way. On your way back, give your partner permission to alter the position or order of your markers to show how she/he sees your story. Then reverse the process. Sit down and talk to each other about what came out of this for you.

5   Sitting in the main circle listen to the music (in this case Bruckner's Sixth Symphony, second movement). When it has finished say whether or not it reminded you of anything. Give your partner permission to tell the others anything about the session you would like to share with them.

6   Turn to your partner and say goodbye in a way that suits you both. Is there a word or a phrase you'd like to give them to take away with them? Then say goodbye to everybody else.

Session three: here and now

We are moving into the central part of the course now. In this and the next session the action concentrates more on the present experience of those taking part. People become more conscious of who they are and what they are taking part in. As before, the leader begins with a short extempore prayer.

1   Standing in a circle throw an imaginary ball across the space to someone on the other side. As you throw it say what your name is. When they catch it they will throw it on to someone else, saying who they received it from but not who they are throwing it to: 'My name is Andrew. I received this ball from Joan and I'm throwing it to *you*.' (at this stage you don't need to know the name of the person you're throwing the ball to, only who it was you 'caught' it from – and they've just told you that!). After a while you will have remembered enough names to carry out the whole process: 'My name is Andrew. I received this ball from Joan and I'm throwing it to Tracy.'

2   Move about in the room finding your own position in it. You are all members of one football team. (Yes, it's a very big team!) Move about in different directions, passing the ball between you. You can shout directions to other players, telling them where you want them

to go. Enjoy the field, the space, the weather, which is just right for the game – fresh and bright, with a slight nip in the air. It's your field, so show off a bit, practise your skills as a footballer – or simply wander about, calling to your friends! Now the game's going to start, so take up your position. How confident do you feel? If you're on top form, put yourself in an 'attack' part of the field, as far away from the safety of your own goal as you can get. If you don't feel as confident as that, find a part of the field suitable for the degree of confidence you are feeling. When you've done this stand there for a moment. Is this where you'd really like to be standing?

3   Sitting in the circle listen to the Bible reading from Luke 14.7–34. Listen to the music. This time it is piano music by Erik Satie, followed by Fauré's *Pavane*.

4   In groups of five or six people make 'living pictures' which represent the way your life is organised at the moment. Each person in the group takes it in turn to cast the others in roles embodying the most important relationships, concerns, joys and sorrows in their life as they themselves see it. (Because you only have four or five people to work with, you must choose very carefully what you want to include in your picture.) Tell the others what it is you want each of them to represent for you and get them to arrange themselves around you to form a living sculpture with you in the centre. Go on to place each person at a degree of distance from yourself corresponding to the relative value and significance of these vitally important persons within your life.

5   In the large circle again. If you want to you can say something about what it was like to do this. As long as you have their permission you may try swapping roles with one of the people you have just been working with so that each of you can address the group as if you were the other person. (People who are really shy sometimes appreciate having someone 'stand in' for them like this!) Now begin to say goodbye to everybody, taking care to let them know that you appreciate their willingness to share with you.

6   Somebody leads off in the conga, dancing round the room in an ever-decreasing circle and ending up with people hugging one another in the crush.

Session four: into the valley

As Easter draws nearer, the feelings and thoughts presented begin to reflect more and more the imagery of the Cross and Resurrection. People's awareness of the liturgical significance of Lent, which has been more or less implicit in the preceding sessions starts to come out into the open. By now, everybody is getting used to a medium that depends on images rather than explanations; acted ideas which take a paragraph to describe in writing but are realised in a few minutes or even seconds in action – 'don't tell me, show me'. Again, the session begins with a prayer, this time the 1662 Book of Common Prayer's Collect for the Second Sunday in Lent.

1   Sitting in a circle ask your neighbours on each side how they have been doing during the week since you last met.

2   Standing in a circle refresh your memory of people's names, using the following game format. You can say the name of the person who is standing either on your right or your left, and they have to answer by saying either your name or that of whoever is standing next to them on the other side. In this way, the succession of names can move either right or left around the circle. In fact, of course it never gets far before someone sends it in the opposite direction by answering their neighbour back (e.g. Gillian, Mary, Gary, Tony, Ikbal, Tony, Gary, Mary, Gillian, etc.). This happens very often, as people soon get tired of simply passing names on and try out various ways of getting their neighbour to reverse order by saying his or her name in a range of different tones of voice – pleadingly, seductively, impatiently, etc. It's a game which provides quite a few opportunities for acting various emotions in ways that invariably cause laughter. If you're not careful it can go on too long.

3   Everybody walks anywhere they want to, taking up all the available space. Try to walk as far away from anybody else as you can manage. Then gradually begin to walk just a little nearer . . . and nearer . . . until you are actually quite close to the rest.

4   Stand in a straight line with everybody else. You are all standing on the bank of an imaginary river. When the leader shouts 'river!', everyone jumps one pace forward; on the command 'bank!', you all jump back. (Your object is to do exactly as the leader says; his (or hers) is to catch you out by giving the same command twice running.)

5   Somebody reads from Mark 8.31–38, 9.1 (The Prophecy of the Passion).

6   Back in the circle sway gently from side to side with your arms round one another's shoulders. Try to find a balance so that you can feel safe doing this and enjoy the gentle motion and the safety of being connected with the group.

7   In small groups talk to the others about a time in your life when you felt weak and discouraged. When everybody has shared, go round the group talking about how it feels to be courageous and strong. Choose two of the stories you've just heard – one about weakness and one about strength – and act these within the group, making sure that nobody feels pressurised to take part if they'd rather just sit and watch. Take time to de-role from the dramas by speaking to the others in the group as themselves rather than the roles they have just been playing.

8   Sitting all together in one circle. Have you anything you would like to share with the whole group? Try to look back on the whole session. Recall it so that you can say goodbye to it and the things that happened in it, until you want to remember them again. So say goodbye to everybody in your own way.

Before the circle begins to break up, the leader reminds people that there are two more sessions to go before Good Friday and Easter. Could everybody bring something next week that reminds them in a personal way of the Easter story? Something they could give to the person sitting next to them?

Session five: supper

1   Walking round the room say hello to all the people you meet.

2   All sitting in a large circle make yourself as comfortable as you can. Form a 'prayer circle' by mentioning someone's name and offering this up to God, along with everyone else. Think of them sitting in the circle with you all and praying with you. The leader announces that there is going to be 'a kind of supper'. Meanwhile have people remembered to bring a gift for their neighbour? If not, they'll have to use their imagination. Certainly everybody present is going to have *something* to take away with them when they leave. Turn to your neighbour and explain what it is that you have brought him or her. (If it is something tangible you can present it to them; you can still do this even if it isn't.)

3   Somebody reads the story of the Last Supper (Matthew 26.26–29).

4   There is music (the Love Scene from Berlioz's *Romeo and Juliet*).

5   In small groups 'The cup of blessing which we bless'. What do these words mean to you? What is it like for you to give things? How do you feel receiving them? If you had a very important gift to give

someone, how would you present it? Try some of these ceremonies out among yourselves.

6   Working all together, put together a ceremony symbolising the search for and eventual discovery of the Holy Grail. (You might want to set up two or more groups to discuss how you are going to do this. Remember, however, that in drama people tend not to know how to do things until they actually find themselves doing them. The courage, and the reward, is in actually taking the plunge.)

7   Back in the large circle take hands and pray together about sharing what we have with others; pray for the hungry people of the world; for those who are sick and in pain; for those who are abandoned and homeless; for any who feel excluded from God's love. In the glory of the Grail pray for a world coming home, a creation restored in Christ. Offer these sessions to God and pray for the continuing guidance of His Holy Spirit. Squeeze hands and shout, in unison 'Goodbye. Go in Peace.' (The rest is up to you.)

Session six: the garden

This final session remembers and also partly represents the garden of Gethsemane. It has a quietness which goes with the idea of a garden – even a so-called 'pleasure garden'. By now these sessions are almost running themselves and the leader's guidance is called on much less than it used to be. This week people tend not to talk very much. They simply enjoy being together and sharing their sadness and hopefulness.

1   In the circle greet one another as warmly as you can, without speaking aloud.

2   One by one walk into the centre where a bowl of water has been placed. Put a pebble into the water and offer a silent prayer.

3   Somebody reads the story of Gethsemane (Matthew 26.36–46).

4   Find a partner (perhaps the person you originally teamed up with in session one). Go with them to a place in the room where you can be more or less by yourselves. Take it in turns to ask each other this question 'would you think less of me if I told you . . . '. Tell them something you have done in your life that you feel ashamed about. Speak as honestly as you can and then listen to what they say. They don't need to say anything at all until you've finished speaking. Now listen carefully as they tell you 'No, I don't think any less of you. Thank you for sharing it with me.' Then you can reverse roles and listen to what *they* will say to you.

5   In the main circle listen to the Adagio of Mozart's Twenty-first Piano Concerto as you join silently in a meditation guided by the leader. (This is about the experience of feeling alone and isolated, drawing on Donne's poem 'To Christ' Wilt thou forgive . . .).

6   Another reading from the New Testament, this time about a different garden (John 20.10–17).

7   In the circle, say a word or a short phrase leading on from what the last person said, to build up a chain of prayer which eventually includes everybody in the group. Then move into the centre of the circle and take up a position showing by means of gesture, bodily position and facial expression, an idea or a feeling drawn from one of the two Bible readings – loneliness and pain for Gethsemane, joy for the other Garden. Join up with the other people to form a 'living picture or group sculpt' expressing both defeat and victory, suffering and deliverance.

8   Move back to the chairs. Sit silently for a few moments. The leader says the First Collect for Good Friday: 'we beseech thee graciously to behold this thy family'.

9   Say goodbye to one another before leaving silently, in the same way that you came.

Chapter 4

Dreaming

I'm climbing the staircase. It's one of the kind that sweeps round like the ones you used to see in Hollywood films, with a great curving banister rail. The stairs are wide and shallow, and there's a fancy candlestick at the top on a plinth. The trouble is, these steps aren't stable, I can't trust them not to give way and land me at the bottom, so I dare not go up any further. Then a voice says keep in at the side. Walk on the shiny part next to the banister. I look up and there's this very old lady standing at the top of the stairs, by the candles. She's really old and her voice is very calm.

This is how C.G. Jung describes archetypes:

Then there is another class of contents [apart from those of personal unconscious] of an origin which cannot be ascribed to individual acquisition. These contents have one outstanding peculiarity, and that is their mythological character. It is as if they belong to a pattern not peculiar to any particular mind or person, but rather to a pattern peculiar to mankind in general. . . . These collective patterns I have called *archetypes*, using an expression of St Augustine's.

(1968: 41)

Jung goes on to say that 'An archetype means a *typos* (imprint), a definite grouping of archaic character.' He explains that he first became aware of their existence when he was carrying out a cross-cultural study of dreams and dreaming. Archetypes are usually associated with the personages who inhabit fairy tales, myths, legends and folklore throughout the world: 'the Hero, the Redeemer, the Dragon (always connected with the Hero, who has to overcome him), the Whale or Monster who swallows the Hero' (1968: 41).

The connection between ritual and dream is a close one; so close in fact, that the species of teaching embodied in the action of corporate ritual 'is like a dream, reflecting the spontaneous and autonomous activity of the objective psyche, the unconscious' (1938: 57). When we are dreaming we are more closely in contact with our spiritual natures than at any other time. In our dreams, as in our rituals, we are lifted outside our ordinary everyday preoccupation with engaging with life in ways that are limited to some practical purpose or other, and are given the opportunity to catch a glimpse of our true selves, and our real objective, the life of spirit.

'It's only a dream.' Only a dream: in other words, vague, insubstantial, over before you have really had time to take it in. In dream workshops we can use ritual as a way of embodying dreams. In other words, we create the special circumstances in which people feel safe enough to explore things about life and death which can be potentially threatening to them.

Dreams need to be embodied rather than simply thought about and 'interpreted'. This is because they are about place as well as time; they present us with a world, not simply an argument, or even just a message. We visit 'the world of the dream'. In rituals this dream world is an actual physical (or even geographical) location that we move into and out of. It is what we experience while we are there that affects our life 'in the real world'; so that, even though we may use the opportunity of being there to act out or stay in narrative which is so important to us, it is the fact of being there that makes it so important – the vision of reality we have that we are there. As James Hillman says 'The primary datum is the image' (1983: 47). It is where our thinking and feeling starts from.

This is why dreams need to be relived; and why we use dramatic and theatrical structure to create a safe place for the encounter with dream reality. Because the most obvious thing about dreams is their fictional nature, the unlifelike quality ('only a dream'), the danger is that we should interpret them by translating what they are saying into a more familiar language, using ideas that are logical and prosaic in order to try to understand them. Presenting them in dream workshops avoids doing this because the experience mirrors the dream experience itself. As Jung pointed out, dreams demonstrate the theatrical nature of human truth, its 'as if' pictorial quality; and they do it by inclusion rather than reasoning. All the workshops described up to now have a dream quality, so that what is said about dream workshops is true to a great extent of group spirituality itself.

In this chapter I shall be giving some examples of workshops designed to provide the structure needed in order to be able to let dreams speak for themselves. In Chapter 1 we were looking at groups themselves, their own native spirituality, going on from there to examine in Chapter 2 the particular circumstances in which they function, the safe space. Chapter 3 was concerned with the task they take on, their purpose and process. Now we will be looking at their underlying subject matter in the dream life of the people involved.

Therapeutic 'dream-time'

Dreams possess a purpose which is psycho-spiritually healing.

In my work as a group therapist I aim to provide the kind of setting in which we can feel safe, both with one another and in the business of being alive together in a shared world. I believe that we need this kind of permission to 'be ourselves'. In most cases, certainly the group members are likely to be feeling more nervous than I am; but professionalism too has its own kind of self-protectiveness, its own wariness about moments of real encounter. So I spend some time making space for us all so that the distance we can establish between us and the world outside may help to reduce the distance that separates us from each other – or at least change its quality so that it becomes less *threatening* and more *interesting*; the fascinating awareness of individuality which draws people into relationship.

These are places and times, set free from the urgent demands made on us by ordinary schedules and locations, in which we can learn to play, practising the real skills we need in order to be a person among persons, in the dream time we have made together.

We have seen in Chapter 2 how the psychologist Donald Winnicott set room aside to play imaginative games with his small client. For her and him, *somewhere else*, 'the back of the room', became a specially privileged location defined by a different kind of awareness – neglected and usually discounted by adults, but as familiar to children as the world in which they are expected to make 'grown-up' sense of life – a place and time which they are only too willing to share with the rest of us so that we may enjoy it too.

We tend to think of this kind of exercise as 'meeting children on their own ground', as if using imagination to expand the boundaries of self-awareness were somehow the prerogative of children, something which represents a necessary stage in their psychological development (which I'm sure it is and does), implying that they will soon grow out of it and be like us, practical and prosaic, with no time for nonsense. Thankfully, however, this is not really the case, or at least not all of it. It was no hardship for the learned psychiatrist to enjoy the freedom and relaxation afforded by the Piggle. Quite the opposite, in fact, the experience calls out to something fundamental to his humanness and which he is only too delighted to celebrate, not only with Piggle and friends, but with us too.

The world of shared imaginative play is a dream world, not because it is substantial and vanishes away when we 'wake up to the realities of life', but because the realities it involves us in are as transparent as dreams. We enjoy them because they give us something denied by our waking world. Something that we really need.

It isn't easy to be precise about what this is, unless you are actually involved in enjoying it, and not even then perhaps. The furniture of this playground world can seem absurdly unrealistic. They are made like this on purpose, in order to suggest the idea of adventure rather than its overtly challenging presence. They are metaphors, aimed at leading us beyond the immediate into the otherwise unmediated. I asked one of my groups to jot down some of the benefits of taking time off to visit such a world and go there as adults.

- In these games you have to have rules, but this is to make it fair. Besides they aren't like the rules you have in life, because they only refer to the game itself. (Rules in real life seem to take you back to being a child, when people had a hold over you and used it.)
- It doesn't matter if you lose, it's only a game: on the other hand it's good to win. It makes you feel better, even though it's only a game.
- Silly games are best. Sometimes we play some kind of board game, which is a challenge. It's OK but it makes me think too hard.
- Games are for all of us who are there. The game is between us. You play it your way, I play it mine, it's the same thing.
- People show what they are really like in a game. I get to know you in a game.

Other things which are the essential characteristics of games are as follows:

- Acceptance and enjoyment of the other person as themselves, the conscious appreciation of their 'otherness'.

- Ability to leave aside the need to understand in terms of one's own preconceived ideas and assumptions (including the carefully constructed, painstakingly referenced impression of myself that I am trying to give).
- Permission to be aware of things one would not ordinarily be allowed to see, or allow oneself to see. Revealing oneself to another person without embarrassment.
- Having something to focus on, a shared experience to refer to during the rest of the time you are together; metaphorically speaking, a place that you have both visited.

This is not a time and space without rules or structure. Each game must have its own rules. It can't be a game without having them – but they are its own rules, constituting its own space. In short, the business of playing games is like that of dreaming. It involves changing the frame of one's mind: I have a conscious intention to break the rules of perception, the reality structure of the waking world. Like dreams, games help us to distance ourselves from a literal interpretation, in which the unbroken succession of events which constitutes our waking lives constitute actual reality and precise truthfulness, and there is 'no room for dreams'.

In the dreamlike circumstances of therapeutic playing, people tell their stories in new ways, not by consciously remembering and recounting the things that happened in an historically accurate way. Here and now they are taken up with what they are playing at, with the special world created by it, in which they can allow the creations of imagination to speak and act on their behalf, not planning beforehand what these people and things will say; by addressing ourselves to the persons in the play, we speak to and about ourselves. What we say may be expounded more or less clearly, in terms of arguments about the meaning of a course of events in the past or the present. It is more likely, however, to be shown in a fascinating, enigmatic way as a transformed and transforming image, something startling which has the power to seize our attention before it clouds over and eventually disappears.

It is this spontaneous improvisatory quality that gives our group sessions their dreamlike nature. It is also, of course, precisely what makes them safe. They are real but not permanent, habitable but not restricting. You can be sad without undertaking the burden of an ongoing depression. You can be angry without cutting yourself off from relationship. You can even be violent without endangering the foundations of your safety. Most important of all, you can hold past and future together in the image

of a present which is inclusive and sufficient. The image contains and embodies the journey.

Rite and dream

> Ritual may be seen as an enacted dream.

It is the fact of embodiment, essential to games which are lived rather than simply thought about that makes the spirituality workshop approach relevant for dreams and dreaming; this and the fact that both workshops and dreams 'speak their own language' in the sense that they create their own formal structures of meaning – their own *rules*. In the world of dreams, these rules are self-consistent, but out of line with the thought procedures of scientific method. This is because their purpose is to describe qualities rather than measure quantities. As we saw earlier, rule systems which are *expressive* rather than *reasonable* are characterised as rituals.

In corporate rituals the action itself articulates a developing argument about the mystical significance of life and death in the form of an image of movement and rest. The gestures and movements of ritual constitute a special language for reliving a special kind of history, one that is both shared and endured and expresses a sense of meaning of things past within the context of their future fulfilment. Carried out in the right spirit, they do not simply remind us of what was done and said in the past, they open our hearts and minds – and consequently our lives – to the promise of transformation. In corporate religious ritual, memory is consummated in the experience of renewal, so that to take part in it involves us more thoroughly and completely in the present. We are enmeshed in the kind of shared world that constitutes real human belonging.

In such a way, by commemorating the past and celebrating the future, the shared rituals which play a central part in these spirituality workshops enrich experience of present reality, just as dreams give resonance to our waking life. They speak the language of embodied human experience, rather than simply requiring an intellectual assent to ideas about the relationship between people and a source of spiritual wholeness. We regard them as basically concerned with our own sense of being alive. In fact, they are not so much states of mind as places we live in.

This makes them extremely powerful. It has been said that 'A ceremonial affirmation, no matter how small seems to carry an indelible and resonant quality into the heart which the intellect is incapable of carrying' (Leunig 1991: 2). Rituals are not ideas we entertain or even truths we assert, but conditions of existence we enter, stay in for a short time and then leave, carrying the experience within ourselves. We regard them as a special way of 'framing' life; and because they are staged in this way they are essentially dramatic; they are public ways of proclaiming human truth in action, little dramas of immense purpose and significance. As dramas, they call upon a parallel rather than an alternative way of construing the world, because they require disbelief to be suspended, not abolished or totally superseded, so that when we take part in them we are actually in two states of mind at once – a perfectly proper place for human beings, because by acting as if our fantasy world were real we give it the truth of our emotional reality and spiritual intention. This is the reality which 'as if' would have if it were really the case; the action of imagining it and living it out in the shared drama imparts this awareness as an emotional reality into our waking experience (Grainger 1995).

Theatre and dream

> The dramatic form assumed by these workshops lends itself to the exploration of dreams, and has a healing effect on traumas sustained in our waking lives.

In plays, audience and actors reach out to one another across the frontier between stage and auditorium. In ritual the meeting is primarily between people and Spirit. In both cases two things mediate the encounter – structure and involvement. As Aristotle pointed out so long ago, the second of these depends on the first, because it is structure that allows us to see beyond ourselves as individuals so that we may distinguish our own personal life from someone else's, the essential prerequisite for being able to form a relationship with them. This is not an easy transaction; it involves moving out from the safety of what is known – and can to that extent be controlled – into what is, as yet, not known, and consequently may turn out to be dangerous. It is the confidence gained from familiar things in life, from the structures we erect and inhabit, that allows us to venture outwards, away from ourselves, in order to make contact with other persons, just as it is their structures, their carefully erected and preserved worlds that stop us from simply taking them over, the place that we think we are safe in, having carefully removed all alien presences, every suggestion of 'otherness'.

The space between these two constructions, our own and the other person's, is demonstrated in drama and theatre, where the gulf is bridged by the agreement to create a new structure, a shared world of embodied imagination. Because the play is safe, because it is and always will be essentially a game, like the therapy games we have just been considering, we can use it as a place in which to unite our personal worlds, turning to one another for comfort, mingling our tears instead of keeping them to ourselves (Duggan and Grainger 1997).

This is how drama uses the human imagination to explore the world of relationship. In dreamlike fashion it allows us to free ourselves from the literal interpretation of life. The absence of any sense of specific instruction – or instructions – being given is basic to drama, which approaches life at an angle, pretending to be talking about somebody else. We are invited to become involved in what is happening and to draw our own conclusions, if they seem to us to be applicable to ourselves. We are engaged in the investigation if we want to be, but we can also remain aloof if we want to. In much the same way we are left free to make sense of our dreams.

To sum up then, both ritual and theatre function by means of the communication of understanding through the transference of feelings. Both are concerned with images of a personal kind which encourage argument and discussion without themselves actually being these things, and are thus dreamlike. Drama, rite and dream work on the same principle, encouraging us to listen without forcing us to listen to what they are saying: they are about life without being part of it in the sense of being subject to the purposes, our own and other people's, which govern our lives. Both ritual and drama serve their own purpose of making dream available, not so much for interpreting as for exploring and living.

In the next section we shall be looking at workshops designed to explore the connection ritual–drama–dream.

Dream workshops

Exploring the dream world

Mythology narrative and dream can be regarded as ways in which we may make contact with psychological realities – psychic presences – that our conscious awareness is directed towards protecting us against or shielding us from. In group spirituality workshops the safe space envisaged in theatre and psychotherapy is realised within a structure that has been specifically devised in order to contain painful meetings of this kind and to embody them in a personal symbolism that we can use to confront the realities of daily life. This is the place and time that we have been describing in this book, the territory which these workshops set out to explore. Here are two basic 'dream workshops'.

I Moving in

1　Walk; don't talk; look; remember. Travel around the room without talking. Acknowledge one another's presence without engaging in any kind of personal contact. Take note of your surroundings – the furniture, decorations, shape of the room, materials used in its construction.

2　Listen to the reading. This is the most flexible part of the workshop. Sit or stand wherever you want in the room and listen to what is being read. (This has been chosen for its evocative and imaginative quality, suggesting the action of leaving one kind of reality for another.)

3　Find a partner and some space where you can be together. Make yourselves as comfortable as possible.

4　Listen to the music together, without speaking. (This has been chosen for the vividness of the images it conjures up and its ability to create a world of its own.)

5　Reflect on dreams you yourself have had – or think you have had – while listening to the music.

6　With your partner, move into a dream either remembered or imagined. Do this in turn, each of you reversing roles with your partner in each dream, and taking a few moments to 'change gear' and come out of role before moving on to the other dream.

7　Sit all together in a circle. Say anything you want about what you've just been doing. (Not everyone needs to speak. People should not feel they are expected to interpret their dreams in any way, but simply to share any insights they would like to put into words. Alternative ways of communicating meaning – drawing, painting, miming, making 'human sculptures' – may be used.)

II Dream-space

1　Explore the space. Discover what it looks, feels, smells like. What does it remind you of? Now encounter the other people in it. What are *they* like? Do they remind you of anything or anybody?

2　Share these memories with a partner. When you have done this find another pair of people to exchange memories with.

3   When you hear the gong, scatter to different points in the room.
4   Settle down wherever you are. Make yourself comfortable and close your eyes. Think about dreaming and listen to the music and the poetry. Don't listen too hard; let your mind wander.
5   Open your eyes now. Can you remember a dream you would like to share with the rest of the group?
6   Take turns to show what your dream was about. You can use the various things we have brought along to do this, or you can show us by re-enacting it. If you want us to help, we'll join in and act the parts for you.
7   Form a circle in the centre of the room and hold one another's hands.
8   Leave your dream behind by telling people who you are. What was the first thing you thought of when you 'woke up'? Share this with the others.
9   Take turns to say what you will take away from the workshop when you leave.
10 Say goodbye to everybody.

That dream again

This is a series of three linked workshops designed to use the safe space afforded by dramatherapy as a way of exploring a particular kind of dream – the recurring nightmare. They took place in a large, warm, comfortably furnished room, where there was plenty of space in which to move around and enough privacy for the people taking part to begin to develop a degree of intimacy as a group who were 'all in it together' (whatever 'it' turned out to be!). In this way, the safe-place metaphor could take on the reality of an actual time and place in which real things could happen to real people, and actual personal changes come about.

In the kind of workshop described here a feeling of safety, of being securely held, is vital. In a dream we may come to a point of extreme terror, a place we cannot think or imagine beyond; but what we actually dream about is the fear of this place, not the place itself, which is hidden from us – what lies round the corner, beyond the doorway, within the cave, etc. What acting out the dream encompasses is the opportunity to confront the fear itself and to do so in a safe environment which will provide us with the ability to do this. The improvised drama provides a framework of conscious make-believe to contain real emotions, allowing them to be lived through 'at one remove'.

This, of course, is the way that drama and theatre work, by catharsis. The release of traumatic feelings which are recognised unconsciously as being too painful and destructive to be consciously registered, by expressing them in ways felt to be safe and non-threatening lies at the very heart of theatre (Scheff 1979; Duggan and Grainger 1997; Andersen-Warren and Grainger 2000). Trauma is German for 'dream': we are released from the power of dreams that haunt us, persistently recurring traumas that revive times and places we thought we had forgotten about, whose power to disturb us we imagined had long since faded away, by acting them through as consciously constructed drama so that they can find their own resolution – in their own language but subject to our power to locate them. This is not a 'fantasy solution' on the part of the individual concerned but a real, social, interpersonal event.

In the workshops that follow, the dream-stories were presented without endings. This is because the dreams themselves had no conclusions, except the obvious one in which the dreamer wakes up in terror or despair. The dream itself, however, finished at this point – the point of waking. Thus, the stories themselves had no ending because it was the ending itself – the true ending which lies beyond the closed door, the cliff edge, the blazing spotlight, the empty living room, the telephone hanging loose on its cord – which cannot be contemplated. Like the awareness that it represents, the dream itself dare not come to its own conclusion. The object of terror, whatever it is that lies beyond, is still being feared within the dream. This, the inhibiting fear, is what the dream is about. We do not dream about what has happened but about what *hasn't* happened yet.

Spirituality groups aim at providing a time in which it can happen in a way that can be tolerated and assimilated. The dream, as we have said, is not the traumatic event itself, or even a picture of that event, but the symbolisation of the fear attaching to it; drama helps these truncated happenings find resolution by reducing the inhibiting tension caused by fears of unimaginable events, thus allowing them to achieve catharsis, or 'emotional purging'.

As we said at the beginning, drama is designed to allow us to be, at one and the same time, observers of and participants in our own personal traumas. The underlying concept is one of balance or emotional symmetry; involvement in the reality of pain is balanced against the distancing effect of imaginative structure. What terrifies me in a dream, giving me no means of escape other than jolting myself back into the waking world, becomes tolerable within the acted scenario, thus allowing me to relax the efforts I have been making to keep it at bay. No wonder I find the experience a peaceful emotional release.

The following three workshops took place on two successive days, Friday evening and Saturday morning and afternoon. There was thus a gap between workshops I and II. This was intentional. Twelve people took part, members of a group of men and women of all ages, 25 years to over 70 years, at a weekend spirituality conference.

I Dream worlds

The leader explains that this is an introductory workshop aimed at giving the group a chance to get used to the basic idea of experimenting with the evocation of a 'dream world' which can be entered and lived in, in company with others. Her instructions are included in abbreviated form. In fact she spent some time explaining exactly what she meant.

1   Find somewhere where you feel you have some personal space. Sit as comfortably as you can. Where would you really like to be? Imagine you're in that special place, wherever it is – in or out of the world – and listen to the music I'm going to put on. Now imagine that you have returned to your place in this room. You have brought something with you to remind you of where you've been. What is it? Place it in the basket in the middle of the room.
2   Choose the nearest person to you in the room to be your partner. Tell them what you have put in the basket and why you decided to bring that particular thing back.

The leader speaks about dreams and dreaming. She reminds everyone that dreams are precious and personal. 'It was *your* dream and *you* had it. In this workshop and the two following ones we shall be exploring this idea together and trying to get inside what it means for us.'

3   With your partner, work out a dream sequence, either actual or invented. Concentrate on how the dream begins and ends.
4   Show the rest of the group what happens in the sequence you have created together. How did you go into the dream? How did you come out of it?
5   Find a piece of paper and something to write with and write down a precious dream that you have had or would like to have. Fold your paper over and put it in the middle of the room so that we have a pile of papers.

The leader asks somebody to make a ring of papers and to leave spaces in between wide enough for people to walk through.

6   Form a circle round the ring of papers and hold hands. Start to dance in time to the music, first in a circle and then in and out of the spaces between the papers. When the dance is over,

7   Find your partner's paper and return their dreams to them. Say 'It was *your* dream and *you* had it.'

8   Say goodbye, first to your partner and then to everyone else.

The leader sets the group an overnight task: they are to prepare for the work they are going to do the next day by trying to remember any dreams they have had which kept coming back from time to time. 'Have you ever been haunted by a dream?'

II Dream-narratives

1   Stand together in a circle. Tell the others what your name is (whether they know or not). Play a game among yourselves in which when the person next to you says your name you have to decide whether to say their name or turn to the person next to you on your other side and say theirs instead. You can only say one of two names, that of the person on your left or on your right.

The ensuing name-battle, as people refuse to break the deadlock between themselves and the person on one side by turning to the person on the other, always makes people laugh and lessens tension within the group. The leader suggests different ways in which people's names can be said: angrily, lovingly, nervously, coyly, etc.

2   Watch and imitate. The leader stands in the centre of the circle and starts to pretend to make herself up, as if for a play. This is done without actual make-up, by miming the various actions as slowly and clearly as possible, and describing what you are doing as you do it. Group members imitate this, making-up the person next to them and then being made-up by them.

3   Divide into groups of four to six people. Choose one from a list of fairy tales prepared by the leader (or decide on one of your own). How does the story go? Work it out amongst yourselves so that you can agree about the plot and characters. Then decide who is going to play what. Leave one person to be the narrator. It doesn't matter how many different parts you have to play; some stories have more people in them than others. Imagine the characters as they will appear when properly made up and in costume.

4   In the group, prepare each person for the part they will play when you present your fairy story to the other groups. Do the same for the narrator, who will need make-up and costume to fit in with the drama.

The groups spend some time doing this. Because they are using imaginary materials, they need to do it as systematically as possible in order not to rush the vital period of preparation.

5   Now present your story to the other groups, acting as audience to them when it's their turn.
6   In your own group, de-role from the character you have been playing. Do this by letting the other group members remove your make-up and help you to exchange the character's clothes for your own again.
7   Find a piece of paper. Write a short letter to the character you have been playing. You can keep this as a memento.
8   Standing in the original circle, talk about what you've just been doing. What did it feel like? Say whatever you want about it.
9   Say goodbye, first to your fellow group members and then to everyone else.

III Dream-meetings

1   Explore the room, making use of all the space it provides. What are its limits – look at walls, ceiling, any nooks and crannies there may be. What kind of furniture is there? What do the windows look out on? Remember what happened here this morning, before you broke for lunch.
2   Journey round the room, imagining different kinds of countryside and terrain that you are traversing. Listen to the leader as she describes the kind of things you have to climb over, push through, wade across, etc. What does it feel like? Use your imagination.
3   Gradually draw closer to the others until you are almost touching, ending up in a tight knot at the centre of the room. Now turn the knot into a hug.
4   Go back into the same groups as this morning. Listen to the music. Is there a dream that you have had several times or keep on having so that you are haunted by it? Talk about it to the others.
5   Choose a dream from the ones described in your group. Now cast

the dream using the members of your own group. (Don't forget to choose a narrator!)

6 Dress and make up the cast and the narrator, as you did in this morning's workshop.

7 Act the dream for the members of the other groups, and be the audience for other people's performances.

8 Remove your fellow group members' make-up and help them put their ordinary clothes back on again.

9 Write a letter to a dream person. This can be someone you yourself have been playing or any of the characters in any of the dreams. Then write a letter to a dream of your own which has been troubling you.

10 Sitting in a circle with everyone else, talk together about the performances you have been taking part in as actors or audience. If you want to you can read your letters out aloud, but you certainly don't have to do this.

11 Listen to the music again.

12 Say goodbye to everybody in your own time. If you want to mention any of the dreams feel free to do so.

This cycle of workshops was specially designed to move slowly and gradually, edging people away from the safety of dreams which they felt they own and are willing to take responsibility for, into nightmares which they cannot get rid of – terrifying implosions of an alien, uncontrollable reality into the fabric of ordinary, everyday living. The dreams as they are acted out go beyond the material presented to become part of a corporate dream experience. In the final workshop described above individuals presented the material as they had experienced it, stopping short at the point of terror when they themselves woke up, terrified into wakefulness by whatever it was that was on the edge of happening to them. At this point, however, the safety of the workshop setting encouraged them to go on, penetrating more deeply into the territory of the dream in order to allow it to reach a tolerable conclusion – tolerable because it was arrived at within the framework of a group game called 'let's play at nightmares'. There was no attempt on the part of the others present to tell the dreamer how to finish the dream. Instead, individual and group moved together to help it achieve its own resolution as something which could be experienced without fear, a whole message instead of a terrifying chaotic fragment.

Nightmares are stories which are too awful for us to finish telling ourselves; and so in our desperation to avoid whatever it is that is coming next we drag ourselves back into the waking world. This, however, is one of the reasons why they are so terrifying, for our peace of mind depends on the things we can make sense of – things with endings in fact. A nightmare is an incomplete message, a sentence without grammar, and as such is already half way to being a message of doom. Let its subject matter concern the things we all try to defend ourselves against, ideas and experiences which remind us of the vulnerability of life and the certainty of death, and the end result is pain and confusion, partly because it isn't the real end but is simply just as much as we can stand. Nightmares, as we saw earlier on, are not about the thing we fear, but the experience of fearing it. When this becomes too intense, we wake ourselves up.

I have kept hold of the notes I made about the first occasion when these three workshops were used. The people taking part had come together for a weekend of dramatherapy. There were nine women and three men, aged between 25 and 70 years. None of them had done this kind of thing before, so that to begin with everybody was nervous and apprehensive. I mention them now simply to give an example of the way recurrent nightmares can be helped to find their own resolution within the special, protected world of the dramatic scenario. Here are four of their dreams.

The actress

Stage fright is a crippling, mind-numbing terror. All actors suffer from it some times and some well-established performers have sought psychological help in dealing with it (Hamilton 1997). Whether or not it is encountered consciously, it certainly haunts every actor's unconscious as a major trauma.

Actress	I can't go on. I shall forget my lines in front of all those people.
Another actor	You must go on. (*He starts to push her onto the stage.*)
Actress	It's no good. I'll die. (*As she is pushed on, she wakes up in terror.*)

This scenario was carried onwards in two alternative versions.

Actress	I can't go on. I shall forget my lines in front of all those people.
Another actress	Never mind – I can't remember *mine* either.

and

Actress	I can't go on, etc. (*Finding herself pushed on stage, she addresses the audience*) I'm sorry, I've forgotten my lines.
Members of the audience	Never mind, love, you can always make them up!

The latter response, coming from members of the audience who were also fellow members of the group, proved cathartic for the protagonist.

The naughty child amuses itself

The main character in this dream-drama was haunted by the presence of herself as a small child. In her dreams she found herself continually being placed at the mercy of this anarchic intruder who was always on the point of breaking in at the crucial point in an adult relationship and destroying it. Then she wakes up.

SCENE I   The child plays by herself, weaving in and out of the pathways in an old-fashioned formal garden. As she plays she talks to herself about the patterns she is weaving.

SCENE II   The adult is talking intimately to her lover. As she moves into his arms, the child bursts in and the moment is irrevocably lost.

This scenario was developed by a scene in which the adult finally takes the initiative.

Adult   Go away – get out of my life forever.

In retrospect it would have been a better solution of the dream problem if she had used the corporate strength of the group to welcome the child in rather than sending it on its way like that. The most important thing, however, is that for the first time in her life she felt able to address the child face to face, and this was obviously a great relief to her.

In the telephone box

The heroine of this drama has a repetitive nightmare in which she finds a telephone box and puts the right money in the phone, but can't get through. She keeps trying, knowing that soon she will have used up all her money. Finally she has to hang up, all her money used and no way of getting through. There is nothing she can do but wake up in distress.

SCENE   A street with a telephone box in it. A woman approaches the box and goes into it. She tries to use the phone, lifting the receiver and putting money in the box, but she obviously gets no reply. She repeats this several times, growing more desperate all the time. Finally she slams down the receiver and bursts out of the phone box in despair.

Woman   I can't get through. They don't answer. I can never get through.

The group carried the scene onwards by ringing her up in the phone box, so that the sound of the bell would draw her back into the box, then, one by one, people spoke to her, thanking her for her efforts to get in touch and saying 'Don't hang up, so and so here wants to have a word with you.' She was overcome with emotion and sank to the floor of the phone box, still holding the phone in her hand. The last group member opened the door of her box and knelt by her, putting her arm round her shoulders.

The dream of the chair-bound man

This is a man who is always very much aware of being the object of other people's attention. When he is in bed at night, however, he feels relieved of the responsibility to play the role of a disabled person. 'Now I can relax and be myself.' At this point, however, he is brought face to face with what 'being himself' means. He dreams that his arm has turned septic; it is gradually getting worse and worse, so that eventually he will develop gangrene and have to have it amputated.

SCENE I   A man is lying on a bed. There is nobody near him, the other people in his life having withdrawn from his presence. The group members are standing as far away from the bed as they can get, and have turned their backs towards it.

SCENE II   The man glances at his arm and looks away again. Then he looks back at it, his attention caught by what he sees. His stare becomes fixed as his horror at what is happening to his arm grows. . . . At this point in the original scenario he jerks himself back to consciousness. In the drama, however, there is more to come.

SCENE III   Seeing their friend's distress, the group members begin to move inwards towards the centre of the room until they are finally surrounding the bed where he is lying. Each of them touches the arm to show him that it is still whole, then they lay their hands gently but firmly on his head. The man lies back and relaxes.

This is what I wrote at the time, trying to recapture the impact of that particular dream workshop. I hope it gives some idea of the kind of thing that happens in workshops like this one, which are real events, integral parts of the lives of the people concerned.

A great many things happen in these workshops which cannot be contained in the descriptions given here. In a way, these are the most important things, the heart of the matter. Like dreaming itself, the workshop is a theatre of the unexpected, which is why it turns out to be so suitable a way of exploring this kind of material. But the discovery is in the doing of it, not the description, which turns out to be much like any other description – the shadow of a reality not the reality itself. Not only its content of images and ideas but the way it works is dreamlike. People say things, do things they literally would not dream of elsewhere. In these workshops the spiritual nature of the relationships involved and of the group itself is dramatically revealed.

The spiritual does not need to be translated or explained any more than dreams do. Because words are incapable of expressing our longing for fulfilment and serenity we turn to our spiritual awareness as to a genuine aspect of our humanity, directing us towards the source of a more complete wholeness. Even though our workshops are not consciously religious they embody states of mind pointing towards religion. To be involved in one of them is to be reminded of humanity's search for truth about life and death, and the closer the involvement the more this search becomes a presence. However game-like they may seem to be, the workshops are concerned with living and dying and with the dream of transcending the limitations imposed by them. Both chaos and order, symbol and narrative embody the struggle for a meaning that is personal and also purposeful.

The dreamlike quality of the approach, in which commonplace ideas and actions carry a significance which continually contradicts their limited everyday usage, is a vital part of their healing power. As with a play, the meaning of a workshop may be taken personally or not, and it is likely to influence the way we think and feel just the same. Through its reverence for natural rhythms it embodies experiences of wholeness in the language of our relationship with other people. Thus, it says things that cannot be said any other way, as gesture and movement pre-empt description, changing human reality in ways that cannot be denied or negated. In the words of Richard Grimes 'The body often understands even against our own desires and thoughts' (1982: 99). This does have to be taken into account even before things that are said. Because it uses people in order to express itself the group workshop is capable of the utmost subtlety of meaning. We learn by involvement with our fellow women and men, and are healed in the event itself, where the drama's ability to bypass our psychological defensiveness and bring us face to face with our own hidden pain is contained within the affirming presence of an accepting wholeness, so that we are caught unawares by the Spirit.

Because its intention is to affect the way individuals and groups experience life in the direction of an enhanced wholeness which is registered as a greater sense of well-being, the spirituality workshop is available as a pastoral resource in all kinds of circumstances. It is personal, flexible, specific; it is also quite easily constructed. This does not mean it can be rapidly assembled or used in a clumsy and absent-minded way. A good deal of investigation must first of all be carried out into the kind of situation it will be used in, which means developing a sense of the kind of material and approach which will fit the needs of individual group members. Every workshop has to be carefully devised in order to address a specific context, with specially chosen music and readings; the only inflexible rule being that the threefold shape of the event must be preserved.

The central section is the hardest part to get right. Here symbols have to be simple yet powerful. Their meaning should be striking in impact without being obvious or trite. This demands a combination of boldness and sensitivity and a genuine concern for the feelings of everybody who will be taking part. Most of all, it depends on openness to inspiration, whatever direction it may come from. If the structure of the happening is preserved, so that the appropriate type of action may take place in each of the three sections of the workshop – setting the scene, working through the drama, de-roling from it – then there is always room for flexibility in the workshop itself; other people's ideas, apart from those of the leader, can bring freshness and spontaneity to the proceedings. You will be surprised at the originality of the things that come out of the workshop – and of course, you will also find yourself knowing the people involved so much better in the process, as you begin to share your own dream-time with theirs.

Chapter 5

Down to earth

Grounding

Life versus dream. The need to establish landmarks.

What the groups aim for is a common place spiritually, one that refers to, and belongs in our ordinary life. In the last two chapters we may appear to have come quite a long way from the place we started off, which was the simple and straightforward idea of a group of people meeting to develop ways of being aware of one another which arise from this kind of shared focusing of attention. We seem to have gone some way towards making the idea of a 'transitional relationship', such as that suggested by Winnicott, appear less ordinary and more exotic than its originator intended. For example, the dream landscapes reproduced in the last chapter represent the furthest point of our journeying inward into the kind of subjectivity which excludes an awareness of others as people who possess the same kind of reality as ourselves, and concerns itself with ideas and figures whose actuality is entirely symbolic – a long way, certainly, from the select human universes we are used to colliding with and rebounding from in any group we can remember belonging to.

At the same time the dream is relevant. Without always knowing exactly what is being said, we do know that this dream is speaking to us about ourselves and the world we really inhabit – the real world in fact. The hard work consists of translating it into the terms which apply to our living reality – the reality of separate persons and shared concerns. The workshop approach lends itself to working with dreams because it allows us to tie them down and share them with others. It is dramatically structured, even when the role we are playing is actually our own, and this, of course, means that it involves us in an interpersonal reality located outside ourselves, in the intervening space our bodies automatically create among us. This is something that cannot be achieved simply by talking about dreams; it belongs exclusively to acting them.

In these workshops, then, we transform the invisible by making it a visible part of the social situation. Just as plays are *about* ideas and feelings, these workshops are about spiritual experience; and they participate in the power of theatre even though they do not involve learning lines or rehearsing roles. The format of the workshop is designed for flexibility and spontaneity. Typically the aim is simply to bring people together in ways that will encourage them to make their feelings, ideas and attitudes available for *interchange* in ways that will avoid the inhibiting effects of direct confrontation, at least in the first stages of the exercise. This is why subjects of intense personal concern are dealt with by projective means involving drawing, painting or clay modelling, or acted out in the guise of somebody else, or simply danced, mimed or even written about.

This indirect approach makes these things available for sharing with others, whereas more orthodox ways of exploring relationships within a group of individuals may not really penetrate to the level at which they could be said to be making real contact with the people concerned. Chapter 1 of this book contains an extract from a 'group member's diary' which mentions some of the emotional difficulties involved in taking part in unstructured groups. Reactions to the dream workshops described in Chapter 4 are very different indeed.

> I admit to being worried about taking part in something I didn't know anything at all about, particularly some thing about 'spirituality', a subject I certainly don't claim to be any kind of expert on. I was also a bit cautious about the 'workshop' too, because it didn't seem to fit the idea of 'spiritual' (not that I'm quite sure what that means). I needn't have worried, though, because the workshop part was really aimed at gently getting us involved in something interesting – I mean, that we were all interested in – and no-one actually mentioned spirituality at all (at least, I don't think they did). Some things we did were extremely interesting, although I couldn't actually tell you what they were. I can remember that people got very involved and moved by things. Perhaps I did too – but it wasn't a problem, as it turned out.
>
> (David, 35-year-old chartered accountant)

I remember more about the workshop as time goes on, as a matter of fact I particularly remember some of the things that other people did and said. (I can't remember what I actually said to them, only what they said to me in reply – so I must have talked quite a bit, too). There are some things that happened which I will never forget, one thing in particular – but I couldn't tell you what it was, not in so many words.

(Julie, 17-year-old sixth-form student)

It was all about dreams, but it was very *real*. A lot of it came to life for me, as if they were my own dreams, not someone else's. Perhaps they were, if you see what I mean. The best way I can put it is that I felt included in a part of myself I don't usually bother about much, don't think really important, not when I'm going about my ordinary life. I usually put dreams and stuff firmly to one side, out of the way. Not necessary; not *real*. Perhaps I shall have to put dreaming back in its proper place again.

(Enid, 60-year-old retired teacher)

I did what I usually do when anyone starts talking about dreams, I suddenly find myself having them, so I couldn't wait to have a go at acting them out. We did actually manage one of mine. It was like receiving a blessing; if you can understand what I mean by that.

(Lisa, 30-year-old actress)

The first thing that comes across from these testimonies is perhaps their vagueness. They are positive, but imprecise. This is because the experience was one of feeling rather than thinking: 'something happened to me during the workshop, but I don't know what it was. I can't tell you exactly because I can't find words for it; but you have to believe me when I tell you that it left its mark in some way or other'. This is because the workshops themselves are *thematic* rather than *propositional*; they don't tell us what to think, but whereabouts to think it, sketching out a general area of experience for us to wander about in, in search of our own meanings and giving us permission to bring back whatever is of interest – whatever it is about our journey that we want to share with others. This is likely to be a feeling rather than a thought; however, in the sharing it may well become a thought, something ready to take its place in the whole network of thoughts and feelings which we use to understand the world (Kelly 1963).

The presence of a theme is a crucial factor in this process of translating emotional experience into personal meaning. Themes may be chosen in advance by whomever it is who has organised a particular workshop or series of workshops, or they may be left in abeyance so that the group can come to its own decision about the subject matter to be worked on. Once chosen, however, they should be faithfully followed through so that their presence is felt at every stage of the workshop process. In a sense, they are that process, because they both originate the movement of the group and define its activity during the period of its corporate life. The group exists to develop its theme, using it not simply as an idea to hang other ideas from, but an experiential focus, in workshop terms, a place to revisit, an area to be re-explored.

The meta-theme

> Dreams filter fundamental truths, offering us chances for change in our attitude to life. These workshops have a similar effect.

There is, however, a propositional dimension to the workshops, and a very important one too. It is that the action of embodying spirituality in this dramatic, experiential way allows us to symbolise the most important human themes of all, those concerning the very terms upon which we are human. Spirituality workshops provide an arena for presenting a vision of life and death. Not simply our ideas about these things but our perception of the qualities they possess. I do not make this claim easily, and I realise that by making it at all I run the risk of appearing facile or insincere. Life, yes perhaps – but death? How can I possibly justify such a thing?

An anonymous contributor to a symposium on 'Spirituality and Healthcare' at Leeds University writes as follows.

> I can no more reflect on the experience of my birth through the conscious recall or memory than I can, at least in the context of this lived life, reflect upon the actual experience of my own death (though most of us will speculate about both of these events at some time or other in our lives).

He (or she) goes on to say that despite this well-established fact, it is possible to dwell on the actuality of other people's dying, and draw 'tentative conclusions' about our own beginnings and endings.

Without any doubt, it is certainly the latter which causes us the most trouble. As La Rochefoucauld said (*Maximés*, Paris, 1665), contemplating one's own death is like trying to look directly at the sun. In spirituality workshops, dramatic identification and symbolic use of people, objects and situations allow us to approach realities projectively, using the medium of the workshop itself to protect us from the immediate pain of presences – and what is more to the point, absences – which would otherwise cause us to look away.

It is amazing, however, the degree of light actually admitted by the dark glasses we put on in order to enter this special world. Generally speaking it is not the intensity of our experience but its quality; our imaginations respond more readily to what is being presented to us because we have been convinced of its harmless nature – harmless to us, that is. We are wrong, of course. Once we have been drawn in we are perfectly capable of perceiving things as if they were happening to us. We see ourselves in someone else's pain and participate in the quality of whatever it is they are imagined to be experiencing, even if it should involve the final abandonment of life. To a greater or lesser degree these shared deaths affect us. They make 'an unspeakable' thing less terrifying by providing us with imaginative experience of dying.

By presenting us with the possibility of personal change and obtaining our conditional assent to the idea, these workshops never fail to bring up the fact of loss, if only the loss of the place we occupy at present, wherever that may be. Loss and change are discovered to be partners – not only of death itself but all the lesser deaths strung out along the road that leads to it. In the workshop these ideas become experiences to be lived and shared – shared in and lived through; an idea of survival which has, through the power of shared imagination, now become an actual experience of life.

Work which touches on such levels needs some kind of preparation, and the need to become really focused on the business of looking at these fundamentals of humanness requires us to take thought about how we are going to 'move into the right gear' for doing so. As we said earlier, anxiety and tension increase defensiveness. The games and exercises which make up the first part of these workshops are designed specifically to overcome the barriers which tend to snap into place when we sense the slightest possibility of anything that might turn out to be emotionally disturbing. The idea is not to deceive but to placate, when we feel comfortable in the presence of the other group members, recognising them as people basically very like ourselves – just as nervous, equally likely to get things a bit wrong and be embarrassed out of all proportion by their own mistakes – an important shift occurs in our feelings towards them. Instead of rivals we recognise them as potential allies, and this is a much more robust frame of mind to be in when it comes to facing up to any emotional challenges that occur during the main body of the workshop.[1] When you have to summon the particular kind of strength we need to allow ourselves to think deeply about our own mortality, or even to be strongly reminded of it, it is a very great advantage to be among friends, people we feel we can trust because we know they share precisely the same group solidarity we were talking about in Chapter 1: it lies at the root of all successful group work and is its most significant contribution to therapy.

Work like this makes use of a variety of different kinds of media, providing opportunities for expressiveness, ranging from structured conversation ('find a partner and spend a few minutes simply talking about such and such a subject'), to role play ('spend a minute or two pretending to be your boss at work'), and actual role reversal ('swap over with your partner so that he/she is you and you are her/him'), to writing letters to imaginary people or receiving phone calls from them and the creation of special environments within the main framework of the workshop as a frame for mime, dance, expressive movement, etc.

These are all ways of encouraging us to 'suspend' our characteristic preoccupation with the outward forms of objects and events – the way things work, what they are used for, the actions they lend themselves to, our reaction to and feelings about these actions, etc. The workshop approach allows us to use our imagination and see the world in a different way. In other words, it encourages us to experiment with rebuilding the world. These experimental worlds may not be real in the actual sense. Indeed, we know very well they are not but the ideas they represent are really ours, and so are the emotions they give rise to, both in ourselves and other people. More importantly still, this action of experiment at reconstruction is in itself a real action. It affects our relationships with other people, the way we and they interact. It is a genuine action affecting reality and is consequently part of it.

And at the same time it affects ourselves, the nature and quality of our own personal reality. The way we see ourselves. We can now see ourselves in a new role, that of co-creator. This is not the way most of us regard ourselves most of the time, as Jonathan Fox points out. It is

---

1   It is always necessary to achieve the right degree of distance, balancing the emotional impact of the material with the feelings of the people involved within the group.

nevertheless the key to our very existence: we are co-creators of reality in co-operation with one another and with God. Much of the time we see ourselves in an entirely different way, as restricted and conditioned, forced into a particular mould by the pressures of life or swept along by a range of dynamisms that we cannot control, either as puppets or victims. Spirituality workshops are one way of countering ideas and feelings like these; they are designed to encourage a sense of creativity, of structures that can be changed and revolutionised, reversed, rebuilt, renewed, and of a self that can be seen to be a participant in the action of changing them. The changes may be temporary, and the reality affected one specially constructed for the purpose, but that is not the point. For an hour and a half or two hours a deeper reality has been revealed, – that of creativity itself, and the stranglehold of the merely factual loosened by debunking things that only seem to be factual, laying claim to a finality which they do not and cannot possess. Only a workshop, only a dream, but the point has been made.

The factor of imaginative participation in group experience, the reflexivity that reinforces selfhood, establishes the understanding that spirituality is now part of 'lived life' and not just a good idea about final meanings. Spirituality workshops open a window into a wider universe than the one which presses down so unremittingly upon us; and they do so by giving us space in which to look at ourselves – at what we are giving and taking; what is between us; what we are co-creating. This in itself gives us something of the courage we need to begin changing our private worlds. As Bruce Wilshire says 'To come to see oneself is to effect change in oneself in the very act of seeing' (1982: 5). In this kind of workshop we are presented with the opportunity to reclaim our identity as relational beings. We 'stand in', and yet also 'keep our distance'. We can do this because of the structure of the group itself; the presence of other people with whom we choose to become involved.

Seeing things differently

> We look back on the experience of taking part in the workshops. What resistances did we encounter?

To return to where we started from. We have covered a good deal of territory during the last four chapters, and in doing so we have, to some extent, reproduced the experience of members of the kind of group workshop described in this book. The workshop experience is essentially one of change and progress. We pass through and move beyond. Every time we genuinely move into something new we have to leave something behind – something of the old reality in which we had invested. When the change involved concerns our spirited identity rather than merely the way we are accustomed to presenting ourselves – our 'worldly' self in fact – it involves a special kind of dying, one willing to take the fact of our own death seriously. This is a dying of self-confidence and defensiveness which opens us up to the challenges of genuine self-awareness; the promise of a more authentic kind of living.

T.S. Eliot captures the emotional paradox involved when he makes his Magi ask if the long painful visit to bear witness to the Messiah's birth had not, in fact, created more problems than it had solved in the way of making any ordinary kind of sense of things.

> were we led all that way for
> Birth or Death? There was a birth, certainly,
> We had evidence and no doubt. I had seen birth and death,
> But had thought they were different; this birth was
> Hard and bitter agony for us, like Death, our death.
>
> ('Journey of the Magi' 1927)

For the Wise Men, the long awaited birth showed itself as an experience of dying that made ordinary living seem insupportable because it could no longer be regarded as in any way *enough*. Some of those who became involved in the spiritual workshops described here have also received more than they had in fact bargained for.

This is something I dreamt last night which really belongs with yesterday's workshop. I was on the island again, my part of the island. (I know it was mine because I recognised the little bush and the place where the little stream was swallowed by the sand – but mainly because I felt it was somehow special to me. This came first – it felt familiar, then I began to recognise the landscape features.) I started to walk into the middle of the island. I felt I'd never really been there, and I had this urge to find out what it was like. The feeling I had to begin with, that it was somehow special, *my* place, stayed with me all the way. In the centre there was a kind of statue – tree – it grew out of the earth like a tree, but it was really a statue, or a kind of monolith. I think it was made out of white stone. It was built over a sort of hole in the ground – actually a crevasse in the white rock under the sand, with its roots clinging to the edge of the space and some lodged in the side of the crevasse. It was holding on, but only just . . . I knew what to do. I picked up the spade (writing about it now I wonder how the spade got there, I certainly wasn't carrying it when I set out.) Now I just picked it up from under the bush and started to fill up the hole. I wasn't frightened or anything although I knew the hole was terrifyingly deep – it seemed to go down forever. I looked over the edge and started to shovel away so that the statue would have somewhere to stand. I was still shovelling when I woke up, so there isn't really a proper ending to the dream. Unless, of course, the shovelling is the ending.

I have to admit that my main reason for coming along was curiosity. When things started to get a bit personal, and we were getting into the sort of areas one doesn't usually mention in public, particularly with a group of strangers – (and I don't mean sex, which actually isn't all that difficult to talk about anyway), things like loneliness and times when you feel really hopeless, as if no-one in the world really gives a damn whether you live or die – and old age and being totally dependent etc., I thought what the hell am I doing here, this isn't my scene at all. It wasn't that anyone was forcing me to talk about this kind of thing, just that the tendency behind some of the stuff that was going on was towards subjects that everybody is a bit frightened of, aren't they? They say that 'when the going gets tough, the tough get going'. I suppose I wasn't tough enough, not for this anyway, and so I got going – in the opposite direction! (If you remember I tried to leave, but the woman I'd been talking to called me back, so I did what she said.) Actually I came back because I didn't want to walk out on *her*, not because I wanted to put myself through any more of what we all seemed to be getting into. I feel I should be honest about this – it wasn't the things we'd been doing that put me off but the thought of where it all might be leading, and whether I would be able to cope. I wasn't keen to put it to the test! When I got back into the group things did get better. I stuck close to this lady and did what she did more or less, even to the extent of playing a part in a play we made up about a teenager leaving home, and the effect this had on her mother (I played her father!). It was very rough and ready, and somebody watching would have thought it pretty daft, I suppose, but I can see the point of it now. It was certainly something different as far as I was concerned, and I shall certainly remember it for a very long time. And not just for the embarrassment, either.

I wrote these two accounts down from memory, so that they represent the kind of thing these two people said rather than a word-by-word record. They are representative of verbal testimonies I have received over the years from a wide range of people who have made contact with the pain at the heart of spiritual transformations and been somehow translated by the experience. The third example, however, is an actual letter received from a group member concerning the group of workshops described on pp. 39–42.

I'm writing to say thank you for the 'spirituality' workshops. I came to all of them, as you probably realise, and I think I gained something from all four – I certainly enjoyed the last one (Workshop IV: Celebrate, p. 42). More than the individual workshops, however, I benefited from the impact of the whole series. You may have noticed that I didn't take a very active part round about the middle of the course. The third workshop, about the labyrinth, was particularly difficult for me. I think this is to do with my having passed through a hard and painful time recently in my own life; I didn't realise exactly how painful it had actually been until I found myself suddenly weeping . . . right there in the middle of everybody. I remember you asking me what was the matter – I think I mumbled something about it being very moving. That is all I said; I was too embarrassed to elaborate.

Well, now I realise, a fortnight and one-and-a-half workshops later, what it was that moved me so much. In one way or another what we were doing reminded me of what life had been like recently for me. I had had to move house and find a new job. It hadn't been easy, and in the middle of it all my Grannie died. Actually I didn't think all that much about it at the time. After all, we were never very close and had more or less drifted apart during the last few years. It was a shock, certainly, and I remember thinking so at the time, but there was just so much going on, so many things I had to do.

One of these, of course, was to let myself shed a tear for Grannie. Let myself feel sad at having neglected her so much recently. Remind myself about her. Just think a bit about her. Well that's what I've been doing. I feel better about her because I have been able to talk to her in my mind. *You* know that we can do that; now *I'm* finding out how to do it, too. It's something I came face to face with in that labyrinth, I know that. I certainly could never have done it before; but then, I never really felt the need, did I? So – many, many, thanks.

The youngest of these three people was in her late twenties and the oldest approaching seventy years old. Most of the workshops, and workshop series, described in the book involved people of various ages ranging from teenagers to octogenarians. Generally speaking this is not an age-specific approach, depending only on the individual's ability and willingness to see her- or himself as a member of a group. Obviously age has to be taken into account with regard to the kind of group envisaged: experimental groups of this kind depend on members' interest in attending to how they and the other members of the group are reacting at any given time to whatever it is that is going on amongst them. In other words, they must be capable of seeing themselves as real members of the group. This means that the factor holding everyone together, a sense of commonality within the group situation is at least as powerful as the tendency to stereotype those who belong to another age group, either resenting or patronising them – certainly refusing to associate oneself with anything they happen to be involved in. The action of identifying a number of people as a social unit bestowing on them a new corporate identity as a group, or even *the* group, does a great deal to defuse the defensively heightened self-consciousness that people of all ages tend to feel when thrown among strangers. Some of the workshops described in Chapter 2 are designed to encourage the change in attitude which must take place before a group of people begins to acquire a new identity as fellow members of a recognisable group.

In my experience, sooner or later the method works even in the most varied and disparate groupings. Individuals who are particularly conscious of 'not belonging' hang back to begin with, but before very long they find themselves drawn further in by the sheer force of wanting to make their personal viewpoint heard by the rest of those present, from which it is only a short step from seeing themselves as a kind of group member – different, individual, but a part of what is going on. As someone said

> I suppose you could say I was never a real group member. I don't think people ever actually saw me as one, either. When I first came, during the first session I thought, what the hell are you doing here with this lot? I just hadn't anything in common with them. I stayed because I was determined not to quit – after all, why should I? I'd as much right there as anyone, and what I wanted to say was at least as important as what they had to offer. Perhaps they'd never come across anybody like me before.

Most groups contain people who feel, or have felt, rather like this. Individuals make their own contribution, however unexpectedly and awkwardly; and it is this awkwardness – and the individuality it expresses – which contributes to group spirituality. The emergence of the spirit in group life does not take place in any straightforward linear way. It involves the coming together of two very distinct kinds of story, the first individual and personal, the second corporate and cosmic. It is out of this meeting that the group's spirituality emerges, giving it its own special liveliness, invigorating its members and pointing beyond itself towards a higher source of unity. We may *intend* a relationship between these two 'narrative realities', but they are very separate, in the sense of being entirely distinguishable from each other. They never simply merge and become a single identity. In group experience, however, they meet, or at least draw close to each other; just as the naturally clubbable people and the stubbornly individual relate with the group structure, so the group's own individuality is drawn into a wider, deeper solidarity than it would enjoy on its own.

Reaching and grasping

Spirituality workshops transmit transpersonal awareness via content and structure.

In Figure 5.1 'story' stands for the personal life narratives of individuals, and STORY for an overarching meaning which belongs to shared, corporate narratives and transpersonal truths.

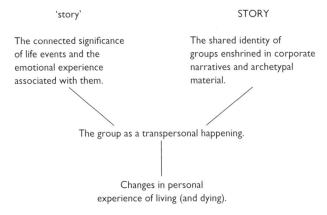

Figure 5.1 Personal and transpersonal story

The structure of personal interaction gives a timeless significance to time-bound experiences and the narratives we use to articulate them. The group itself is symbolic of a wider truth, in the sense that by structuring itself for the express purpose of sharing experience it becomes a spiritual organism, a 'body with many parts'. Having an identity and purpose inseparable from those possessed by its members but brought nearer to the source of its spiritual life by its willingness to participate in the action of sharing. The good of its spirituality is a wholeness and unity in which individuality and self-expression achieve their ultimate transformation in what might be described as a condition of mutual inclusivity (Wilber 1981).

The most striking visualisation of this kind of unity of selfhood is the Jungian archetype, the transpersonal symbolism of aspects of life and death which are intensely personal in the sense of being communicated to individuals in ways that correspond to their own unique selfhood, while resonating with a truth which applies to the entire human race. The archetype which corresponds most closely to the kind of group holism we have been talking about is the mandala, the 'primordial image of psychic totality'. This is the pictorial form taken by the *coincidentia oppositorum*, involving the transformation of opposites into a higher synthesis – not merely personal differences or expressions of individuality but actual opposites! In the words of Joland Jacobi 'Whenever this symbol, which can manifest itself in the most divergent forms, makes its appearance the balance between the ego and the unconscious is restored' (1962: 131).

As the archetypes of order, mandalas represent the relationship between two unities, the human and the divine by including them in the image of a superordinate unity. Jung himself spoke of the mandala as appearing spontaneously in dreams and works of art 'as a compensatory archetype, bringing order, showing the possibility of order' (Jung, cited by McGuire and Hull 1978: 328).

No wonder then that workshops of this kind contain so many invitations to the people taking part to 'form a ring in the centre of the room' or 'go back to the wider circle'. In these workshops the image of a superordinate unity is continually invoked, and done so without any conscious awareness of the spiritual significance of things which are really quite ordinary. The symmetrical shape of the workshop itself, arranged as it is around a central phase of heightened emotional involvement which serves as a point of balance for the structure as a whole; the use of stories which have a beginning, a middle and an end; expressive or ritualised movement and dance; carefully chosen music of a rhythmic or formal kind – all of these are ways of symbolising an ideal heaven or perfection which is able to speak the language of the soul. To this extent, spirituality workshops are acted mandalas, symbols of a perfection which, however expertly we may realise its imagery, will always be outside our reach and yet never cease to refresh us in the action of reaching for it.

The sense of meaningful form transmitted by, and embodied in, the workshop itself not only expresses a yearning for wholeness and spiritual fulfilment, it also reveals an awareness of the actual presence of spiritual truth. In this way the workshop is a genuine symbol of the perfection it has to mirror. It is vitally important however, to stress that this does not depend on how well it is carried out. The value of the play *as a play* in no way depends on the skill of the actors performing it. In one way our expertise may actually get in the way. We are concerned here with a fundamentally unactable drama, a perfection which may be reached after but never grasped. It is vitally important that this should never be forgotten, even for a moment; the authenticity of what we are setting out to do depends on it. In reproducing the imagery of a transcendent perfection we are not trying to conjure it up. There is no idea of control here, no element of manipulation. Our spirituality as human beings consists in our need to draw near to the source of our life which is also our hope of perfection.

Marie-Louise von Franz describes the mandala as 'a symbolic representation of the nuclear atom of the human psyche, whose essence we do not know' (Jung 1964: 213), any more than we possess intellectual understanding of the Being of God. This psychic imagery mediates kinship, not identity, and the danger is that we might, in our own cleverness, confuse the two things, ending up with a form of magical thinking which is at the opposite pole to spirituality. It is the beyondness of God, the reaching out to the transcendent which is vital, for it is in searching for, rather than capturing, that our authentic spirituality is revealed.

The congruence between earth and heaven is symbolic, never literal – but the symbolism is of wholeness, a state of affairs in which the two realities can somehow meet and mingle. Mandalas are about the interpersonal situation here on earth. The imagery of the wholly related serves to focus the relationship between people within the group. In 'the *quadratura circuli*', the square on the circle or the circle in the square, the imagery of separation and the imagery of mutuality are combined to make up 'the symbolism of wholeness' (Jung, cited by McGuire and Hull 1978: 327).

It is the experience of similarity-in-difference that characterises real group belonging. From inside the group our awareness is expressed as

'I', 'you', 'we', 'they', but never simply 'us'. To this extent the differentiated solidarity of the group brings the transcendent home to those taking part at every stage of the workshop. Certainly at some level, conscious or unconscious, every group does this, because each of them is both an image and example of shared personhood. Groups that come together to explore their sense of spiritual values certainly 'have heaven in view', that is, the achievement of a heightened sensitivity towards 'the Other' however they may actually describe it. The spirituality workshops described here are designed to focus a very positive yearning for transcendence, which can be powerfully disruptive of ordinary attitudes about acceptable ways of behaving in the company of others.

In religious ritual the mandala symbolism acts as a shield as well as a mirror reflecting transcendence and at the same time protecting us from its full, intolerable impact (Jung 1983). Real inspiration seems to demand this kind of caution, being quite able to override our ordinary civilised – in the sense of restrained – behaviour, a fact that the uninspired find disconcerting or even downright alarming. In these workshops we dance in circles, avoiding undisciplined movement, and present our drama safely in role, our intention being to draw near to the presence of joy with some respect for our own human vulnerability and weakness.

And yes, of course, people do become excited and enthusiastic; and other people are put off by their enthusiasm. The connection between the excitability of social gatherings which so impressed Durkheim (1915) and the tendency of therapeutic groups to regress into 'childlike and primitive behaviour' noted by Bion (1961), is explained by the heightened emotional impact of group structure, in other words the combination of formalised procedure and highly emotional content that allows people taking part to give vent to feelings which are usually kept under rigid control. The discovery that these feelings are shared by other people within a structure which has actually been designed for their expression can lead to vivid experiences of empowerment!

> I shall never forget being on that island with everybody. I don't know how to describe what it felt like. I was entirely alone and yet totally joined with everyone else. It was like freedom happening in a game with rules – like things *should* be.

> I've felt peaceful before of course, now and again, and sometimes it has happened with one particular person, now and again. But never with a whole group, nine or ten other people. Somehow you feel very strong when that happens, very confident.

At first I just stood on the edge and looked in. I could see what people were doing, but not why they were doing it. They were all very involved, and that put me off, of course. At the time I remember, I wasn't very keen on getting involved with anything, particularly anything new. So you could say I was resisting this – I couldn't see the point. Later on, though, after I'd done the mime about the dove (I did it because no-one else seemed willing to try) I felt entirely different, and then I began to see the point – or what might possibly be the point. It's something about actually doing things and not just thinking about them with your imagination; actually getting inside things and doing them. Quite simple, really.

I can't really dance, you know, and I don't think there were all that many of us who could – especially the men – but it felt as though we were dancing on the floor of heaven.

People tell me I'm an intellectual, perhaps because of my scientific background. Anyway I just think of myself as a logical thinker. I like things to add up. So what happened over this weekend has left me almost completely wordless. I can't analyse what was going on, but something certainly was, and I feel quite differently about things because of it. Differently about myself, differently about other people. I'm still thinking it out, puzzling over what actually happened. Was it helpful? Yes it was. How? I don't know – ask me later, will you.

Recreation and re-creation. *Working with creation stories*

Spirituality workshops are vehicles for creativity as well as messages about it. This is demonstrated in the experience of working with certain myths.

In Chapter 1 we looked briefly at the psychoformative effect of simply playing, and particularly of playing *together*. We saw that dramatic play, depending on as if reality, proceeds directly out of this, because of the impulse to explore the experience of living together with our fellow human beings by trying life out for size in the safe space of shared imagination. Some kinds of psychotherapy are inherently dramatic, for example psychodrama (Moreno 1969; Blatner 1997), dramatherapy (Jennings 1987, 1992; Jones 1996; Andersen-Warren and Grainger 2000) and gestalt therapy (Perls, Hefferline and Goodman, 1973), none of which can really be understood except by reference to what happens in drama and theatre. According to Antonucci-Mark, psychoanalysis itself functions within a fictionalised frame in which therapist and client join in 'an interplay of fantasy and reality, past, present and future thoughts, feelings and emotions' (1986: 14; cf. also McDougall 1986). Psychological theories whose exploration of life takes account of the category of the spiritual – post-Jungian transpersonal psychology (Hillman 1983; Grof 1979; Wilber 1981) and psychosynthesis (Assagioli 1975) for example – see imaginative playing as a way of bringing the human soul and spirit into communion with the creative forces of the universe.

The theme of creation, both human and divine, and the relationship between the two, constitutes the fundamental subject matter of spirituality workshops. In so far as these workshops are concerned to make the unseen seen, embodying the imagery of between-ness and beyondness, they are symbolic of the original creative action whereby the universe itself came into being. Our creative imagination does more than simply imitate the divine action, it actually participates in it, as the essential characteristic of our createdness. This means that to imagine is, for us, to be real. As Jean-Paul Sartre says 'The imagination is not a contingent and super-added power of consciousness, it is the whole consciousness as it realises its freedom' (1972: 217). To create is to experience the freedom of being. 'It is because he is transcendentally free that man can imagine' (Sartre 1972: 216). No wonder those whose imaginations became engaged in the workshops described here, report a feeling of authenticity. The things imagined were real enough, because the imaginary is 'the "something" concrete toward which the existent is surpassed' (Sartre 1972: 217).

In the language of religions these imagined experiences are real because they participate in the original creativity of God. The *Deus Faber* of ancient Egypt was believed to dwell in the myth-creating faculty of human beings. Marie-Louise von Franz (1995) records a creation myth of the African Basonge, according to which the highest God, Mwile, quarrels with Kolumbo mui fange 'the one who made himself', he who has been created now demands the right to be in charge of creation himself. Similarly, an African Basonge creation story describes an argument between the originator of life and the son he has made for himself: 'N'kolle said "I have created everything!" Fidi Mkullu said "No, I have created everything!"' (1995: 134, 100). The similarity of such myths to the biblical story of Adam and Eve is obvious.

It is a question of a series of genuine new beginnings. Imaginative creativeness – creation in the image of God – is not limited to whatever may have already happened. In the world's creation myths we are concerned with the renewal of life not by modification or even restoration, but actual *re-creation*. Mircea Eliade quotes M.S. Stevenson's *The Rites of the Twice-Born*, with regard to the Fijians.

> Each time that life is threatened and the cosmos, in their eyes, is exhausted and empty, the Fijians feel the need for a return *in principilo*. Hence the essential importance in rituals and myths, of anything which can signify the 'beginning', the original, the primordial.
>
> (1971: 19)

The instinct to create, then, is actually the need to re-create or at least become involved in a process of re-creation.

Wherever these creation stories originate they tend to reveal these two characteristics.

1 The idea of total newness and originality. An example of this would be the Apatak myth in which the creator of all life, Tulungersaq, or Father Raven, first of all actually creates himself 'He sat crouching in the darkness when he suddenly woke to consciousness and discovered himself' (von Franz 1995: 29). In this way, to use Sartre's phrase, his 'existence was surpassed' in an action of freedom and self-expression that was both infinite and total.

2 The theme of 'creation', our co-operation with the source of life; the human and the divine working together for the perfection of a shared reality.

The creation myths of the world offer many opportunities to explore this theme to benefit from its power to revive the 'imagination that makes us free'. This is not simply a rethinking about life but a rebuilding of a world; and we, as men and women, are involved in it, in the action of re-creation itself.

> There is a beautiful tale among the Australian aborigines which says that the bow and arrow were not man's invention, but an ancestor. God turned himself into a bow and his wife became the bow-string, for she constantly has her hands around his neck, as the bow-string embraces the bow. So the couple came down to earth and appeared to a man, revealing themselves as bow and bow-string, and from that the man understood how to construct a bow. The bow ancestor

> and his wife then disappeared again into a hole in the earth. So man, like an ape, only copied but did not invent, the bow and arrow. And so the smiths originally . . . did not feel that they had invented metallurgy; rather, they learned how to transform metals on the basis of how God made the world.
>
> (von Franz 1995: 141)

Creation myths and stories tend to follow a pattern which is probably as ancient as the human race itself, that of 'a triple statement, in the form of a repetitive rhythm within the narrative', three sisters, three caskets, three wishes, followed climactically with a fourth event which performs the function of a final, decisive, hammer blow, transforming a thrice-told tale into the mandala of a perfect action; story; *truth*. Among the Maidu 'Earth Initiate' is held to create the world using earth fished up by the tortoise. He grasps this in his hand

> and rolls it about until he has a lump as big as a little stone, which he puts on his raft. From time to time he looks at it, but it does not get bigger until he looks at it the fourth time. Suddenly, it becomes as big as the world.
>
> (von Franz 1995: 249)

The hammer blow is not just decisive, it is in fact conclusive. Creation myths do not simply tell us how a particular story ended, they signify the final destination of all stories, and story tellers, too, leaving us full of awe at the significance of a creation which calls for such an ending as this.

These stories of the beginning and end of all things have left their mark – their structural imprint – on all kinds of stories, everywhere in the world. As we saw earlier, the action of organising the things that have happened to you, and that you yourself have done, into the form of a connected narrative is a spiritual action in itself, expressive as it is of your own personal reaching out towards meaning and significance for your life. The form your action takes relates directly to the underlying shape of these creation myths, as this has been conceived as the archetype of meaningfulness, the order of things, whether they are sounds, colours, shapes, textures or events in a story, which will provide us with a material symbol of ultimate perfection.

In some way these stories stand out as subjects for the kind of spirituality workshops described in this book. It would be hard to imagine better ones, in fact. They must, however, be allowed to speak for themselves, without adaptation or distortion, because as we have seen, their unique expressiveness, their message, in fact subsists in the characteristic of *interior balance*. They need to be enjoyed with respect for their true nature as spiritual truth. Movement, mime and dance may be used in order to convey the sense of symmetry which characterises the narrative; but there is no way of revealing the living spontaneity of the Spirit's presence by skill alone. What these workshops must depend on – the only things they can depend on – are the creativity and freedom whose message they are transmitting.

Creation workshops

The following workshops leave more room for imagination than some of those described earlier. Their main outline, however, remains the same.

I   Introduction – preparation. We explore ways of making ourselves feel relaxed and alert.

II Action – the myth itself. This, the main business of the session, will develop as it goes along. We listen to the story and then portray its meaning.

III Closure – de-roling. We stand back from the actions performed and parts played within the symbolic world of the story. Is there anything we would like to share with the others? We meditate for a minute or two, then say goodbye.

I Introduction

There are no instructions for these workshops, not, at least, at this stage of the proceedings. It is impossible to provide a blueprint for something which is meant to turn out differently on every occasion. The aim here is to present a story in ways that express its meaning to those presenting it; and the only way to do this is by discovering what that meaning is! The only thing that can be done in advance is to make some attempt to prepare the ground for the kind of soul exploring which is going to take place here, no one yet knows how; and this is the purpose for the section I have called introduction.

II Action

The action part is yet to be revealed, however. This is the part which, every time it happens, does so for the first time. This could be said about all the workshops in this book of course, but up to now I have sketched in various bits of supportive framework in order to provide a platform for people's imaginations to take off from. Not with these workshops though.

These are workshops about creation itself. We are looking at the way things are created and, by implication, our own share in creating them. In other words, if we plan them out in advance we have already created something, if only a plan of some kind; but isn't the planning an important part of what we want to explore? What we do have already, however, is ourselves, one another, and whatever it may be that is happening among us. We are, after all, searching for a way in which we ourselves can present the idea, experience, event of creativeness. We may as well start where we are. Talking to someone is a creative act, maybe *the* creative act in some ways, so is touching them or even simply looking at them.

People work on this in pairs or small groups, or all together in the larger group. They also work by themselves, and on how it feels to be alone. There are no rules for working in this way so long as what is happening feels free to those concerned, thus expressing the creativity which is the message of the story. The story's theme is ultimate creativity, and this is the inspiration for the workshop.

This is why this approach – in which all sorts of new ideas are tried out and old ones adapted to fit – is the only practicable way of demonstrating the reality it describes. Creativity allows itself to 'take several bites at the same cherry'. It is willing to make mistakes and to pass through stages of indecision and uncertainty (see Workshop I, p. 36), when it doesn't know which way to turn. Creativity dares to lose itself in chaos, only to re-invent itself there. In a story about invention, the workshop approach could scarcely be improved on.

In these workshops, things can be used as themselves or made to stand in for something else; space is allowed to become flexible, stretched out or collapsing in on itself, likewise time; horizontal planes may be used to signify vertical ones, so that climbing is demonstrated by walking. Anything in the room is available for transformation, or just for ordinary construction purposes. The visible can be drawn, painted, modelled; invisible things can be described, shown by gesture or expressive movement, or sung about.

Most important of all, people can exchange roles and the illusion accepted as an important, perhaps crucial, reality. Actions and incidents can be rehearsed or performed spontaneously, included in a presentation for other people, or experienced as part of a drama in which everyone in the workshop is an actor and all share in a liturgy that all have helped to create.

The thing to be avoided is any suggestion of trying to produce a slavish copy of the original, although this would be a temptation. It would certainly be a move in the wrong direction so far as encouraging creativity is concerned. Enjoyment, interest, fun are all more objective than copying. The way we arrive at original insights, ideas that are new to us, is certainly not by concentrating as hard as we can on the task of thinking them up. Quite the reverse. In fact it turns out to be better to think in terms of Alice's garden, a mandala designed precisely to illustrate this point – that the only way to reach the centre of things is by walking outwards towards the circumference! Linear thinking and creature discovery are in fact poles apart, the latter depending, in Koestler's words, on 'a de-differentiation of thought's matrices, a dismantling of its axioms, a new innocence of the eye, followed by liberation from restraints "in order to allow" a re-integration in a new synthesis' (1977: 5). Our thinking needs to be loosened so that it can be constructively refocused elsewhere (cf. Kelly: 1963).

When they are confronted by something as carefully designed and perfectly balanced as a creation myth, group members need encouragement to persist in following their own ideas and feelings, even if what they produce may appear to be a good way away from the myth as this was read out to them. This indirect approach allows the symbolism of 'original creativity' to work away behind scenes until it is ready to reveal itself to the group as an authentically new version of itself, to be compared with and enjoyed alongside the other one.

> Finally, overall advice for this part of the workshop would be to allow yourself to relax into it. Try to immerse yourself in the creative process so that the workshop itself begins to work for you. There is no right or wrong way of doing the things suggested here; although it should be said at once that trying too hard is certainly wrong, whereas accepting absence of inspiration usually turns out – in the end – to be temporarily right. Once you start enjoying what you find yourself doing you warm up, and the ideas start to emerge, heaven knows where from!

III Closure

The content of this will, of course, depend on what has been happening during the main 'myth making' section. Its main business concerns the need to allow ourselves to return home from the journey we have been making together. When we explore ideas and feelings in this dramatic way we exchange aspects of ourselves – joys and sorrows, frustrations and satisfactions, strengths and weaknesses – with the roles we take on in the story we are allowing ourselves to become involved in. This section is intended to be an opportunity to draw conclusions from the difference between the role being played and the person who is playing it: and for the person themselves to share her or his experience of the drama with everyone else involved in it. The whole workshop ends with a short time spent silently together.

These workshops are instances of the group's use of what Jung calls 'active imagination'

> He who speaks in primordial images speaks with a thousand voices; he lifts the idea he is trying to express out of the occasional and transitory into the realm of the ever-enduring. . . . That is the secret of effective art.
>
> ('Contributions to Analytical Psychology', 1928, cited by Jacobi 1962: 24)

'Creative power', Jung says, is mightier than its possessor. Its mightiness comes primarily from the images it invokes and realises. Spirituality workshops of this myth-based kind bring us into contact with this primal imagining and enlist our own creativity in active ways in its service. We are involved in order to be used, as creators of spiritual truth not merely creatures from it; although it is because we do draw our wisdom as human beings from this great well of archetypal understanding that we are able to contribute to it, as we use our knowledge of the world we inhabit to transmit our awareness of a deeper reality. Spirituality workshops are rarely presented as works of art; but because this kind of approach permits people to experience their own and others' creativity, they may be regarded as active promoters of spiritual truth.

Four creation myths

Hupi (North American Indian)

Begochiddy, the earth god, created the world. First he made four mountains below the world, with four different kinds of ants (and also some bugs), and planted bamboo in the mountain of the east. This was the first world.

When the bamboo had grown up, a hole was made and all the inhabitants of the first world climbed up and through the hole. When they had gone Begochiddy pulled the bamboo up into the second world, and Hashjesjin blew into the hole four times to make it close up. The first world burned up after them (and is still burning). Begochiddy created new mountains in the second world just like the ones in the first one. He planted white cotton in the East, blue in the South and so on. The men women and creatures then went on to climb into the third world.

Here Begochiddy and the other gods created another world for people animals and insects to live in, again the inhabitants leave, en route for world number four. This however is entirely covered with water, and so is inhospitable. With the aid of the locust, who has broken up through the crust covering the third world in order to discover what is waiting above, the people come into the fourth world and settle there.

(Adapted from Franz 1995: 54, 55)

Hindu

The God Vishnu once took the form of a tiny minnow. The minuscule glimmer of the swimming god caught Manu's eye. Instantly, the First Man scooped it up in one hand.

To save the divine fish from predators larger than itself, Manu kept it alone in a water dish. When it outgrew the dish he transferred it to a jar, then to a barrel, then to a pool, then to a pond, then to a lake and finally to the ocean, since by that time Vishnu had grown sufficiently great in girth to swallow any other fish.

Long afterwards a great flood arose, inundating the shores of the world. As Manu ran away inland, the billowing surge overtook him and swept him far backwards down the watery abyss. He would have drowned, but Vishnu – who was now Leviathan – arrived in time to save him. So Manu rode out the flood in comfort on Vishnu's back, which seemed a sizeable floating island, a Paradise, or a New World rising when the old had disappeared.

(Eliot 1993)

Maori (New Zealand)

Io dwelt within breathing-space of immensity.
The Universe was in darkness, with water everywhere.
There was no glimmer of dawn, no darkness, no light.
And he began by saying these words, –
That He might cease remaining inactive;
'Darkness, become a light-possessing darkness.'
And at once light appeared.
He then repeated these self-same words in this
    manner, –
That he might cease remaining inactive;
'Light, become a darkness-possessing light.'
And again an intense darkness supervened.
Then a third time He spake, saying:
'Let there be one darkness above,
Let there be one darkness below (alternate).
Let there be a darkness unto Tupoa,
Let there be darkness unto Tawhito;
It is darkness overcome and dispelled.
Let there be one light above.
Let there be one light below (alternate)
Let there be light unto Tupoa,
Let there be light unto Tawhito.
A dominion of light,
A bright light.'
And now a great light prevailed
Io then looked to the waters which compassed him
    about,
and spake a fourth time, saying;
'Ye waters of Tai-kama, be ye separate,
Heaven, be formed' Then the sky became suspended.
'Bring forth thou Tupua-hero-nuku.'
And at once the moving earth lay stretched abroad.

                              (translation in Sproul 1991)

Salinan Indian (North American)

The Old Woman of the Sea was jealous of Eagle and wished to be more powerful than he. So she came towards him with her basket in which she carried the sea. Continually she poured the water out of the basket until it covered all the land. It rose nearly to the top of the mountain where were gathered Eagle and the other animals. Then Eagle said to Puma, 'Lend me your whiskers to lasso the basket.' He made a lariat out of the whiskers of Puma and lassoed the basket. Then the sea ceased rising and the old woman died.

Then said Eagle to Dove, 'Fetch some earth!' Then Eagle made the world of the mud brought by the dove. Then he took three sticks of elder and formed from these a woman and two men. But still they had no life. They all entered the sweat-house. Then said Prairie-Falcon, 'Fetch my *barsalilo!*', Coyote went to bring it, but brought a load of different wood. 'No!' said Prairie-Falcon. 'That is not my *barsalilo*,' and Coyote had to go again. Then they all sweated. After sweating, the eagle blew on the elder-wood people and they lived. Then they made a bower of branches and held a great fiesta.

(J.N. Mason, from Sproul 1991)

Appendix

Rites of passage

The spiritual workshops described in this book follow a pattern characterising ceremonies of change and renewal throughout the world. Everywhere, corporate ritual expresses our sense of moving through life in terms of actual physical movement. In rites of passage 'The passage from one social position to another is identified with a territorial passage, such as the entrance into a village, the movement from one room into another or the crossing of streets and squares' (Hamelin 1972). This is the essence of drama, involving us in actual personal experience and not simply informing us about abstract truths – however important they may be. It is also the essence of ritual, as we offer the terms of our daily existence to the divine course and completion of life. It takes place in a human setting, but its purpose is to embody our experience of God. Because it concerns the whole person in an inclusive way, its ability to change exceeds that of any argument.

Certainly the most vivid illustration of this is the rite of passage. Here a religious doctrine concerning the emergence of life from death is presented as a dramatic narrative which initiates those taking part into a new, higher condition of life. In cultures throughout the world, liturgies of transformation are used to crystallise our human perception of the significance of every development, expected or unexpected, which occurs to us in the course of our lives, using the shape of events to move us into the presence of God. Such rituals give shape to our stories by presenting them in terms of a final story, one which embodies divine perfection. In the actions used to bring this about we are spiritually transformed – conformed to the divine image. In other words these rituals speak to us in a highly personal way, using our own imagery to reveal what lies on the other side of the final threshold, where the flux of becoming is the perfection of Being. We are conscious of 'leaving' the world in one state of personal being and 'rejoining' it in another, having been changed by our journey.

Rites of this kind may be used to bestow a special kind of significance on events and situations, contact with the source and goal of life giving rise to an experience of newness which inspires those taking part to embark on a new stage in their journey. This is the initiatory action which Eliade distinguishes in all corporate ritual. The need for it is 'co-existent with any and every human condition' (1965: 128). From time immemorial it has given shape to human life, modelling its own interior and exterior organisation on biological, psychological and social changes occurring within life, and acting as a kind of midwife to states of affairs which need the type of public recognition and divine authority that it alone can give. Such rituals are particularly useful with regard to states of affairs which involve pain and suffering; when the present is unacceptable to us and we would like to ignore it completely or pass over it quickly and move into a more acceptable future. Rites help us to 'grasp the nettle' of change.

The phrase 'rites of passage' was first used by the Dutch anthropologist, Arnold van Gennep. He describes them in this way: 'A complete scheme of rites of passage theoretically includes pre-liminal rites (rites of separation), liminal rites (rites of transition) and post-liminal rites (rites of incorporation). . . . To cross the threshold is to unite oneself with a new world' (1960: 10). By a process which depends on an experience of separation from the rest of society, a consequent period of isolation and disorganisation, and a final time of incorporation within a new personal and social world, candidates for social and religious change are delivered from their old way of being into one which is experienced as authentically new. In order to understand how this can be done we need to remember some of the things we mentioned in Chapter 3, when we were looking at stories and story telling.

In any story there must be some kind of climax, an event that encapsulates the action simply because the story pivots on it. It is in fact the principal reason for telling the story at all, in the sense that the conflict brought about by the need for change of some kind has created a situation which must somehow be resolved. There must of course also be a starting point, both in order to locate the story in the ordinary course of events, and to signal the point at which it departs from this. And there must be an ending; without a consummation there is no point in bringing up the subject in the first place.

However, in sophisticated story telling, these three elements do not necessarily follow each other in the order followed by the original events on which the story is based; part of the skill of story telling consists in the way events are presented, so that frequently we have *stories-within-stories* – 'flash-backs', false climaxes and ambiguous conclusions. The fact remains, however, that virtuosity of this kind is only effective because it is not really successful. These things work because we are never fully convinced by them. They keep us searching for the underlying order by which the story's message is communicated, a course of events which has a real beginning, middle and end.

It is the rite's triple shape that brings its message home. This is the inalienable shape of transformations that are not simply thought about but experienced. Real change is never a simple distinction between old and new, former and latter. For real change to take place, the old situation must really end, and the new one really begin, which means that there must be an element which is neither old nor new, but different from both. This point between is difficult to envisage with any clarity, so long as we content ourselves with simply thinking about it. It is how things are after the old state of affairs has ended, and before the new one has begun. Thus, the outer movements of the rite frame the central section which, like the centre of the turning wheel, produces and receives movement without getting anywhere itself. How can it if it is the epicentre of the conflict which lies at the heart of every real change, and the motive power which drives the workshops described in this book.

At the same time we have to take account of the fact that this moment of between-ness is in fact always the present moment. Our hope for the future is not in 'before' or 'after', but in 'now'. Because we are always engaged in remembering the past and anticipating the future we have no real psychological grasp upon the present, which is the point at which we actually live. In fact, however, the future does not come to us from the past. It comes from *now*, the experience which eludes us, yet is nevertheless where we are, the space we inhabit.[1]

---

1   We are tempted to think dyadically about the things we experience because our mental comfort seems to require us to classify all we perceive in terms of discernible differences. Our way of arranging what we experience into manageable, assimilable groups depends on the action of separating *this* from *that*. There are some things we cannot do this with, however. From time to time the threeness of things demands attention. Perhaps it is worth taking a little time to consider the significance in human thought of things that are threefold. For the Greeks, three was the perfect number; more than this, it represented the invariable number of components necessary for an action that would be perfect or express perfection. This was quite a practical consideration; because it had a beginning, a middle and an end, such an action would possess its own integrity, and could stand

In ritual of any kind, and most dramatically in rites of passage, we arrive at the true threshold only in the middle of the rite, not a moment before. Real thresholds are always difficult, even painful. In the language of religious ritual, the pain is inherent in the process of dying and rising again, leaving behind all that is known and loved and trusted, in order to face things that can only be thought about in terms of an insupportable absence.

In passage rituals of the kind described by A. van Gennep (1960) and V. Turner (1974), this inevitability of pain is brought home by experiences deliberately intended to reveal it by externalising and amplifying its presence. For the initiand, past and future are abolished by the urgency of what is going on here and now. This agony is contrived, like everything else in the rite; it has been systematically rendered unforgettable.

In fact, the rite functions to make us aware of what is really involved in change for human beings, with their tendency to cling to the vain belief that they can somehow switch from a totally familiar state of affairs to one that is completely strange without having to go through anything at all in between, changing their lives with the same facility that they can change their minds. Even when, perhaps *particularly* when, the change is one that concerns our life at a deep level, we would rather get on with the business of getting used to the new state of affairs before we have any real knowledge of what it consists of; before it has come into existence in fact. Stranded between a world that has died and one that has

for itself. Thus all authentic propositions, every opinion that its proposer would be willing to vouch for and able to defend, would be of this kind. Synthetic propositions, in which the opposition of the first two parts are triumphantly resolved in the third one, are more powerful than ever. Even if we content ourselves with saying the same thing three times over the effect is considerable, however, 'Like the computing machine, the brain probably works on a variety of the famous principle expounded by Lewis Carroll in *The Hunting of the Snark* – "What I tell you three times is true".' (Weiner 1961: 154) The cumulative effect of triplicity is apparent everywhere, not only in literature – where the simple threefold story provides the basic narrative foundation of novels and plays, and folk tales and fairy stories depend on three wishes, three suitors, three dangers or perils to be faced, three brothers or sisters competing to face them – but in ordinary life, where entertainers receive a round of applause the third time they say something, which, when said for the first time was greeted with almost complete silence, and teachers and politicians get their message across by remembering the time-honoured advice 'Tell them you're going to do it, do it, and tell them you've done it.' The *doing* is the most difficult, of course, just as the second delivery of a running gag, receiving the least response, provokes the most anxiety. In these threefold forms the central section bears the weight of meaning because it has to come to grips with the problem, embrace the agony of change and cast loose from its supporting structure.

not yet been born we are lost and dismayed. In the state of mind which is neither one thing nor another we do not know what to think, how to feel. We try to bypass our own pain by moving into a fantasy future, which has all the naturalness and familiarity of the world we are used to, being in reality only an ersatz extension of that world. Thus, by imagining we can move from one thing straight into another, we are defeated by the process we thought we were mastering.

There is, then, a vital stage in human change that we prefer to ignore and consistently try to avoid. Change is always a process rather than a unitary event, revolving round a central experience of very great significance, which we may choose to ignore but whose action we cannot escape. The effectiveness of any kind of ritual in realising this stage and overcoming our tendency to elude it, governs its effectiveness as an instrument facilitating change. In threefold rituals of transformation, the facts about human change are articulated within a recognisable human happening, defined by a beginning, a middle and an end, in which the two outer movements draw attention to the importance of the central section by 'framing' it. There is no glossing over of the crucial centre ground, which is the psychological reality of change itself as distinct from mere wishful thinking. By involving us in an experience which conforms to the preconditions of a real-life transition, ritual educates us about our own personal growth, which necessarily involves pain and which we would rather avoid.

Ritual takes us into a place and time we cannot sustain, and then leads – or carries – us out again. This is a place we hardly dare contemplate because its demand is so extreme. To describe the tendency to avoid taking it into account as leaping over the grave is no exaggeration. Every real human change involves, and must in some way have been recognised as, a genuine dying experience. So that the new may live, the old must really be known to have died. Rites of passage exist in order to help us take account of this vital fact.

Thus, in rites of passage throughout the world the median 'liminal' phase makes extensive use of the symbolism of death as an effective way of putting pressure on life as we are used to living it. Such rituals aim at changing the way in which individuals perceive the world itself. Even though they are experienced in concrete ways, their message draws its power from religious metaphor rather than literal statement, as physical movement and bodily gesture point away from themselves to what is, apart from the use of symbolism, inexpressible. The action does not have to be as violent nor the experiences involved so painful as they are in the ceremonies described by cultural anthropologists and historians of religion (cf. Eliade 1965; Turner 1974). People involved in spiritual workshops do not have to endure actual bodily mutilation or sensory deprivation designed to sever their links with the past by flooding their awareness with the pain of an insupportable present. The underlying principle, however, remains the same. Fears that are not normally faced, ideas and feelings that tend to give us pause are more powerful in their effect, more real in their significance, than we assume them to be. For those personally involved, the presence of things that summon up realities which they would prefer not to contemplate renders the liminal phase a challenging place, a time of trial to be undergone. Which is why the final part of the workshop is designed with the specific purpose of invoking the symbolism of reassurance and belonging.

Epilogue

Once upon a time a group of people met together in order to try to explore what it really meant to be human. Once upon a time . . .

In these workshops we start with a story, not as an idea or an argument, but as a place to move about in. We move into the space it makes and find out what happens in it. The room where we are becomes the place where it lives.

It may be a school room or a village hall, it may even be a church. But whatever or wherever it is, it is inhabited by the story, a beckoning presence in a world as wide and deep as our imagination. Normally, of course, we make sure it will know its place by imprisoning it in our notebooks or nailing it to a clipboard so it may have no chance of escaping our critical intellect or expository fervour. No chance at all. The stories we hear and read in church, sitting quietly and obediently in our pews or standing perched behind the lectern, appeal to our church selves. They communicate with the church side of our awareness. We tell ourselves how very much we love them – but one way or another we still manage to emasculate them.

Spirituality workshops give them room to breathe. In the liturgical space that we allow ourselves they come and live amongst us, reaching out to us and inviting us to take a walk in their world and see how readily it becomes our own. In a sense they create this space for us and in us, as they expand our imagination to meet their world. In the workshop we do not simply encounter this imaginative reality, we are able to move into it and explore it in the way we make sense of the world we live in. In other words, we embody it. We talk about making sense of what we hear, but we usually take this to mean that we interpret them, organising them into ideas we can assimilate. In this case, however, we mean something different. To embody is to make bodily sense of an experience not simply perform a cognitive operation upon it; to move into it; to inhabit it.

You use your imagination. Nobody tells you what to do. You listen to the story, imagine the space and *move in*. Whatever liturgy emerges from this kind of experiential workshop is a liturgy of movement. In the most immediate way of all it is story-become-liturgical action. Theological reflection follows this instead of preceding it. People who take part have a feeling of discovery, of having actually been somewhere. Perhaps this is because they haven't been given any idea about what they will find (or, in the case of normal church procedures, what they have expected, what they must find).

The people who have been coming to these workshops have something of a problem describing them to their friends. They say they can't forget them, and yet somehow they can't remember them either.

> Someone asked me what it was like, what we did, and do you know I couldn't tell him. And it's been like that all along, ever since the first session ten weeks ago. I can never remember what we actually do at all. All I know is that when I leave I seem to carry away with me a great sense of peace.

And isn't that a kind of knowledge? A very deep kind?

Bibliography

Adler A. (1980) *What Life Should Mean to You*, (first pub. 1932). London: Allen & Unwin.

Aldridge D. (2000) *Spirituality, Healing and Medicine*. London: Jessica Kingsley.

Allport G.W. (1955) *Becoming*. New Haven: Yale University Press.

Andersen-Warren M. and Grainger R. (2000) *Practical Approaches to Dramatherapy: the Shield of Perseus*. London: Jessica Kingsley.

Antonucci-Mark G. (1986) Some Thoughts on the Similarity between Psychotherapy and Theatre Scenarios, *British Journal of Psychotherapy* 3: 1, 14–19.

Artaud A. (1970) *The Theatre and its Double* (trans. V. Corti). London: Calder & Boyars.

Assagiolo R. (1975) *Psychosynthesis*. Wellingborough: Turnstone Press.

Bailey E. (1997) *Implicit Religion in Contemporary Society*. Den Haag: Kok.

Bailey E. (1998) *Implicit Religion: an introduction*. London: Middlesex University Press.

Benson J. (2001) *Working More Creatively with Groups*. London: Routledge.

Binswanger L. (1956) Existential Analysis and Psychotherapy. In F. Fromm-Reichmann and J.L. Moreno (eds) *Progress in Psychotherapy* New York: Grune and Stratton.

Bion W.R. (1961) *Experiences in Groups*. London: Routledge.

Blatner A. (1997) *Acting-In*. London: Free Association Books.

Bly R. (1992) *Iron John*. Reading, MA: Addison Wesley.

Brook P. (1968) *The Empty Space*. London: MacGibbon & Kee.

Buber M. (1957) *Pointing the Way*. London: Routledge.

Buber M. (1961) *Between Man and Man*. London: Collins.

Buber M. (1966) *I and Thou*. Edinburgh: T. & T. Clark.

Bugental J.F.T. (1967) *Challenges of Humanistic Psychology*. New York: McGraw-Hill.

Campbell A. (ed.) (1987) *A Dictionary of Pastoral Care*. London: SPCK.

Coleridge M. (1908) *Poems*. London: Elkin Matthews.

Corey. G. (2000) *The Theory and Practice of Group Counseling* (5th edn). Pacific Grove, CA: Brooks/Cole.

Cox M. and Theilgaard A. (1987) *Mutative Metaphors in Psychotherapy.* London: Tavistock.

Crites S. (1986) Storytime: Recollecting the Past and Projecting the Future. In T.R. Sarbin (ed.) *Narrative Psychology.* New York: Praeger.

Des Pres, T. (1977) *The Survivor.* New York: Pocket Books.

Douglas T. (1993) *A Theory of Groupwork Practice.* London: Macmillan.

Dowling-Singh K. (1999) *The Grace in Dying.* Dublin: Newleaf.

Duggan M. and Grainger R. (1997) *Imagination, Identification and Catharsis in Theatre and Therapy.* London: Jessica Kingsley.

Durkheim E. (1915) *The Elementary Forms of the Religious Life.* (trans.) W.J. Swain, London: Allen & Unwin.

Elam K. (1988) *The Semiotics of Theatre and Dance.* London: Routledge.

Eliade M. (1958) *Patterns in Comparative Religion.* London: Sheed & Ward.

Eliade M. (1965) *Rites and Symbols of Initiation.* New York: Harper & Row.

Eliade M. (1968) *Myths, Dreams and Mysteries.* London: Collins.

Eliade M. (1971) *The Myth of the Eternal Return.* Princeton: Princeton University Press.

Eliot A. (1993) *The Global Myths.* New York: Penguin Meridian.

Epictetus (1983) *The Handbook.* (trans.) N.P. White. Indianapolis, IN: Hacket.

Erikson E. (1965) *Childhood and Society.* Harmondsworth: Penguin.

Fay P.P. and Doyle A.G. (1982) Stages of Group Development, The Annual Conference for Facilitators, Trainers and Consultants. San Diego, CA: University Associates.

Foulkes S.H. (1965) *Therapeutic Group Analysis.* New York: International Universities Press.

Fox J. (1987) *The Essential Moreno.* New York: Springer.

Fox M. (1983) *Original Blessing.* Santa Fe: Bear & Co.

Franz M-L. von (1995) *Creation Myths.* Boston: Shambhala.

Freud S. (1930) *Civilisation and the Discontents.* C.W. Vol.21. London: Hogarth Press and Institute of Psychoanalysis.

Fulgham R. (1995) *From Beginning to End.* New York: Rider.

Gennep A. van (1960) *The Rites of Passage* (trans.) M.B. Vizedom and G.L. Caffee. London: Routledge.

Goffman E. (1986) *Frame Analysis.* Boston: Northeastern University Press.

Gorman C. (1972) *The Book of Ceremonies.* Cambridge: Whole Earth Tools.

Grainger R. (1988) *The Message of the Rite.* Cambridge: Lutterworth.

Grainger R. (1990) *Theatre and Healing.* London: Jessica Kingsley.

Grainger R. (1995) *The Glass of Heaven.* London: Jessica Kingsley.

Grimes R.L. (1982) *Beginnings in Ritual Studies.* Washington: University Press of America.

Grof S. (1979) *Realms of the Human Unconscious.* London: Souvenir Press.

Hamelin J-Y. (1972) 'Les Rites de Passage', Maison Dieu No. 112 (own translation) pp. 133–143.

Hamilton L. (1997) *The Person Behind the Mask.* Greenwich, CT: Ablex.

Heron J. (1998) *Sacred Science: Person-centred Inquiry into the Spiritual and Subtle*. London: PCCS Books.

Hillman J. (1983) *Healing Fiction*. New York: Station Hill.

Hopewell H. (1988) *Congregation: Stories and Structures*. London: SCM Press.

Jacobi J. (1962) *The Psychology of C. G. Jung*. London: Routledge.

Jennings S. (ed.) (1987) *Dramatherapy, Theory and Practice for Teachers and Clinicians* vol. 1. London: Jessica Kingsley.

Jennings S. (ed.) (1992) *Dramatherapy, Theory and Practice for Teachers and Clinicians* vol. 2. London: Jessica Kingsley.

Jones P. (1992) Lecture Notes (unpublished), Hertford College of Art and Design.

Jones P. (1996) *Drama as Therapy, Theatre as Living*. London: Routledge.

Jung C.G. (1938) *Psychology and Religion*. New Haven, CT: Yale University Press.

Jung C.G. (1964) (ed.) *Man and His Symbols*. London: Aldus/Jupiter.

Jung C.G. (1967) *Memories, Dreams and Reflections*. London: Collins.

Jung C.G. (1968) *Analytical Psychology: the Tavistock Lectures*. London: Routledge.

Kelly G.A. (1953) *The Psychology of Personal Constructs*. New York: Norton.

Kelly G.A. (1963) *A Theory of Personality*. New York: Norton.

Kierkegaard S. (1959) *Either/Or*. Vol. 1 (trans.) D. Swenson and L. Swenson. Princeton: Princeton University Press.

King W.L. (1954) *Introduction to Religion*. New York: Harper & Row.

Klein M. (1997) *The Psycho-Analysis of Children*. London: Vintage.

Koestler A. (1977) Regression and Integration. In W. Anderson (ed.) *Therapy and the Arts: Tools of Consciousness*. New York: Harper.

Larson D.B., Swyers J.P. and McCullough M.E. (1997) *Scientific Research in Spirituality and Health: A Consensus Report*. Rockville, MD: National Institute for Healthcare Research.

Lawrence D.H. (1971) *The Complete Poems of D.H. Lawrence*. V. de Sola Pinto and Warren Roberts (eds). New York: Viking Penguin.

Leach E. (1976) *Culture and Communication*. Cambridge: Cambridge University Press.

Leunig M. (1991) *A Common Prayer*. Oxford: Lion.

Lewis G. (1980) *The Day of Shining Red*. Cambridge: Cambridge University Press.

Macmurray J. (1933) *Interpreting the Universe*. London: Faber.

Marcuse S. (1984) *Freud and the Culture of Psychoanalysis*. London: Allen & Unwin.

May R. (1975) *The Courage to Create*. London: Collins.

May R. (1983) *The Discovery of Being*. New York: Norton.

May R.M. (1993) *Cosmic Consciousness Revisited: the Modern Origins and Development of a Western Spiritual Psychology*. Rockport MA: Element Books.

McDougall J. (1986) *Theatres of the Mind, Illusion, Truth on the Psychoanalytic Stage*. London: Free Association Books.

McGuire W. and Hull R.F.C. (eds) (1978) *C.G. Jung Speaking*. London: Thames & Hudson.

Mead G.H. (1934) *Mind, Self and Society*. Chicago: Chicago University Press.

Merleau Ponty M. (1962) *The Phenomenology of Perception*. London: Routledge.

Miller W.R. (ed.) (1999) *Integrating Spirituality into Treatment*. Washington DC: American Psychological Association.

Moreno J.L. (1937) *Sociometry*, vol. 1. New York: Beacon House.

Moreno, J.L. (1969) *Psychodrama* vol. 3. New York: Beacon House.

Nitson M. (1996) *The Anti-Group*. London: Routledge.

Oatley K. (1984) *Selves in Relation: An Introduction to Psychotherapy and Groups*. London: Methuen.

Orchard H. (ed.) (2000) *Spirituality in Health Care Contexts*. London: Jessica Kingsley.

Pannikar R. (1973) *The Trinity and the Religious Experience of Man*. London: Darton, Longman & Todd.

Perls F.S., Hefferline R.F. and Goodman P. (1973) *Gestalt Therapy*. Harmondsworth: Penguin.

Poewe K. (1999) Conversion Among Charismatics. In C. Lamb and M.D. Bryant (eds) *Conversion*. London: Routledge.

Rähner K. and Vorgrimler H. (eds) (1965) *The Concise Theological Dictionary*. London: Burns Oates.

Rank O. (1958) *Beyond Psychology*. New York: Dover.

Rich A. (1978) *The Dream of a Common Language*. New York: Norton.

Rogers C. (1967) *On Becoming a Person*. London: Constable.

Rogers C. (1969) The process of the basic encounter group. In J.F.T. Bugenthal *Challenges of Humanistic Psychology*. New York: McGraw Hill.

Rogers C. (1970) *Encounter Groups*. Harmondsworth: Penguin.

Romanyshyn R.D. (1982) *Psychological Life from Science to Metaphor*. Milton Keynes: Open University Press.

Rose J. (2002) *Sharing Spaces?* London: Darton, Longman & Todd.

Rowan J. (1993) *The Transpersonal*. London: Routledge.

Rowan J. (2000) Humanistic Psychology and the Social Construction of Reality, *Psychotherapy Section Newsletter British Psychological Society* 29: 1–8.

Sarbin T.S. (ed.) (1986) *Narrative Psychology*. New York: Praeger.

Sartre J-P. (1972) *The Psychology of Imagination*. London: Methuen.

Schechner R. (1988) *Performance Theory*. London: Routledge.

Scheff T.J. (1979) *Catharsis in Healing, Ritual and Drama*. Berkeley: University of California Press.

Schreur A. (2001) *Psychotherapy and Spirituality*. London: Jessica Kingsley.

Scott N.A. (1971) *The Wild Prayer of Longing. Poetry and the Sacred*. New Haven CT: Yale University Press.

Sheldrake P. (2001) *Spirituality and Theology*. London: Darton, Longman & Todd.

Slade P. (1995) *Child Play*. London: Jessica Kingsley.

Sperry L. (2001) Spirituality in Clinical Practice: New Dimensions in Psychotherapy and Counselling. London: Brunner-Routledge.

Sproul B.C. (1991) *Primal Myths*. San Francisco: HarperCollins.

Streng F.J., Lloyd C.L. and Allen J.T. (1973) *Ways of Being Religious*. New York: Prentice Hall.

Sullivan H.S. (1953) *The Interpersonal Theory of Psychiatry*. New York: Norton.

Swinton D. (2001) *Spirituality in Health Care*. London: Jessica Kingsley.

Thorne B. (1997) Spiritual Responsibility in a Secular Profession. In I. Horton and V. Varma (eds) *The Needs of Counsellors and Psychotherapists*. London: Sage.

Tillich P. (1962a) *The Courage to Be*. London: Collins.

Tillich P. (1962b) *The Dynamics of Faith*. London: Collins.

Tuckman B.W. (1965) Developmental Sequence in Small Groups, *Psychological Bulletin* 63: 384–399.

Turner V. (1974) *The Ritual Process*. Harmondsworth: Penguin.

Vaughan F. (1985) *The Inward Arc: Healing and Wholeness in Psychotherapy and Spirituality*. Boston: New Science Library.

Washburn J. (1995) *The Ego and the Dynamic Ground: a Transpersonal Theory of Human Development*. Albany: State University of New York.

Weiner N. *Cybernetics, or Control and Communication in the Animal and Machine*. Quoted in M. Gardiner (ed.) (1961) *The Annotated Snark*. Harmondsworth: Penguin, p. 46 n. 2.

Whitaker D.S. (2001) *Using Groups to Help People*. London: Routledge.

Wilber K. (1980) *The Atman Project*. Wheaton: Quest.

Wilber K. (1981) *Up From Eden*. London: Routledge.

Wilber K. (1982) Conversation. In K. Wilber (ed.) *The Holographic Paradigm and Other Paradoxes*. Boston: Shambhala.

Wilber K. (1985) *No Boundary: Eastern and Western Approaches to Personal Growth*. Boston: Shambhala.

Willows D. and Swinton J. (eds) (2000) *Spiritual Dimensions of Pastoral Care: Practical Theology in a Multi-disciplinary Context*. London: Jessica Kingsley.

Wilshire B. (1982) *Role Playing and Identity*. Bloomington: Indiana University Press.

Winnicott D.W. (1971) *Playing and Reality*. London: Tavistock.

Winnicott D.W. (1980) *The Piggle*. Harmondsworth: Penguin.

Wright A. (2000) *Spirituality and Education*. London: Routledge.

Yalom I.D. (1970) *The Theory and the Practice of Group Psychotherapy*. New York: Basic Books.

Yalom I.D., Miles B.B. and Lieberman M.A. (1973) *Encounter Groups: First Facts*. New York: Basic Books.

Afterword

Our selfhood can be, by turns, both citadel and prison. Secure within its walls we perceive ourselves to be protected from that which might seem to threaten our identity. At the same time, those walls can so easily close upon us, inhibiting the full discovery of that identity.

And yet, as the author reminds us, our true spiritual reality transcends this kind of separate identity. 'No man is an island' and so, in the mutually agreed suspension of reality which the group dynamic permits, members are – by happy paradox – set free to venture beyond the walls of self to risk a deeper exploration of reality: free to encounter the Beyond in their midst; and free to experience the creative embrace of the God in whom we live and move and have our being.

Archbishop of York

Index